CAMBRIDGE LIBRARY COLLECTION

Books of enduring scholarly value

Literary Studies

This series provides a high-quality selection of early printings of literary works, textual editions, anthologies and literary criticism which are of lasting scholarly interest. Ranging from Old English to Shakespeare to early twentieth-century work from around the world, these books offer a valuable resource for scholars in reception history, textual editing, and literary studies.

Chawton Manor and Its Owners

Chawton House is famous today as the home of Jane Austen's brother Edward, who was adopted by a wealthy relative, Thomas Knight, and inherited his Hampshire estate. Edward offered the former bailiff's cottage close to the great house to his mother, who lived there with her unmarried daughters Jane and Cassandra. The house is now a study centre and library, for women's writing especially, but when this book was published in 1911 the building was still the Knight family home. Montagu Knight, the grandson of Edward, supplied material from the archives of the manor, while the book was largely written by his cousin William Austen Leigh, the son of Jane's nephew and memorialist. It covers the history of the manor from the Norman Conquest to the death of the second Edward in 1879, and, apart from the Austen connection, is a fascinating illustrated history of a typical English parish.

Cambridge University Press has long been a pioneer in the reissuing of out-of-print titles from its own backlist, producing digital reprints of books that are still sought after by scholars and students but could not be reprinted economically using traditional technology. The Cambridge Library Collection extends this activity to a wider range of books which are still of importance to researchers and professionals, either for the source material they contain, or as landmarks in the history of their academic discipline.

Drawing from the world-renowned collections in the Cambridge University Library and other partner libraries, and guided by the advice of experts in each subject area, Cambridge University Press is using state-of-the-art scanning machines in its own Printing House to capture the content of each book selected for inclusion. The files are processed to give a consistently clear, crisp image, and the books finished to the high quality standard for which the Press is recognised around the world. The latest print-on-demand technology ensures that the books will remain available indefinitely, and that orders for single or multiple copies can quickly be supplied.

The Cambridge Library Collection brings back to life books of enduring scholarly value (including out-of-copyright works originally issued by other publishers) across a wide range of disciplines in the humanities and social sciences and in science and technology.

Chawton Manor
and Its Owners

A Family History

WILLIAM AUSTEN LEIGH
MONTAGU GEORGE KNIGHT

CAMBRIDGE
UNIVERSITY PRESS

CAMBRIDGE
UNIVERSITY PRESS

University Printing House, Cambridge, CB2 8BS, United Kingdom

Cambridge University Press is part of the University of Cambridge.
It furthers the University's mission by disseminating knowledge in the pursuit of
education, learning and research at the highest international levels of excellence.

www.cambridge.org
Information on this title: www.cambridge.org/9781108076210

© in this compilation Cambridge University Press 2014

This edition first published 1911
This digitally printed version 2014

ISBN 978-1-108-07621-0 Paperback

CHAWTON MANOR

AND ITS OWNERS

Geo Romney   Cath: Knight

Emery Walker Ph.sc.

CHAWTON MANOR

AND ITS OWNERS

A FAMILY HISTORY

BY

WILLIAM AUSTEN LEIGH
FELLOW OF KING'S COLLEGE, CAMBRIDGE

AND

MONTAGU GEORGE KNIGHT
OF CHAWTON

WITH PORTRAITS AND ILLUSTRATIONS

LONDON
SMITH, ELDER & CO., 15 WATERLOO PLACE
1911

NOTE

ALTHOUGH my name appears as that of one of the authors, my share in this book has consisted mainly in the collection of materials to be put into their present shape by my cousin, whose name stands first on the title-page.   In the collection of these materials I have received invaluable aid from my wife.

MONTAGU G. KNIGHT.

September 1911.

CONTENTS

ILLUSTRATIONS

PORTRAITS

ILLUSTRATIONS IN THE TEXT

BOOK PLATE OF THOMAS KNIGHT

CHAWTON MANOR AND ITS OWNERS

CHAPTER I

EIGHT CENTURIES

T is told of a celebrated historian who flourished in the Victorian age—more celebrated, perhaps, for picturesque statement than for patient investigation—that he was once turned loose in the library of an old house particularly rich in manuscripts dating from the period with which his work was specially identified.

identified.   Between each bookcase round the walls of the room were carved oak pilasters.   The historian was directed to one of these pilasters, the front of which opened and disclosed a rich treasure of documents bearing on his studies.   These he examined with some care ; but when he was told that the cupboard behind this pilaster was only a specimen of what was to be found behind every pilaster in the room, his heart failed him, and he declined to carry his researches further.   It is possible that the future historians of England—those especially who are occupied in describing the social and economic conditions of the country—will find themselves in a like manner overburdened with the information provided, whether in manuscript or in print, by the numerous family chronicles of the present date.   But, after all, nothing can be so useful, either for imparting valuable information or for correcting hasty theories, as accounts which give typical instances of individual villages and families.   We need not, therefore, scruple to add our small mite to the store which is growing on all sides ; for among the typical instances to which we have alluded Chawton can fairly claim an honourable position.   The beauty of the situation, the venerable age of the Manor House, the old-world character of the village, and its literary associations ; the fact that the property (though it has been owned by members of several families) has only once since the Norman Conquest changed hands by way of sale and purchase—all these advantages give the place a peculiar title to be considered as a specimen south English manor.

Our

Our plan is to give in our first chapter a brief *résumé* of the history of Chawton and its various owners, and afterwards to descend into particulars, grouping them under the following headings: (1) Manor, (2) Church, (3) Manor House and Families of Owners.

Chawton may be said to be in the valley of the Thames, as it is placed on rising ground near the sources of the Wey. The form of the place-name in Domesday Book, ' Celtone,' makes it improbable that it has anything to do with the chalk which, mixed with clay, brick-earth, and gravel, abounds in the parish. At one end the Manor runs into the immediate neighbourhood of the green sand; while, for timber, the whole area is rich in beeches, oaks, and elms. The village stands about one and a half miles distant from the town of Alton, at the point where the main roads leading respectively to Winchester and to Gosport separate. Just on the junction stands the small house where Jane Austen passed the last eight years of her short life. At the further end of the village, on the Gosport road, stand the Rectory on the right hand and the Church on the left, and, on the rising ground behind the Church, the old Manor House. Behind the house rise still further the garden and shrubberies, and at the summit of the hill a terrace commands a view over the Church to the high beech woods on the western limit of the parish, known as Chawton Park. The place is not far from the great world, and there are several residences of some size in the village; but the verdure, the luxuriance of timber, and the

the absence of any buildings obviously new, give to the
casual visitor the idea of a home deep in the country, and
the impression is strengthened by a longer stay.   There is
no reason to doubt the continuance of the conditions
which produce this impression, if only travellers to Alton
will possess their souls in patience, and abstain from endeavouring to induce the London and South-Western Railway
to increase the very moderate speed of their trains on
that branch.

   There are several curious analogies between the history
of Chawton and that of another old place in the North of
Hampshire, viz. the Vyne, near Basingstoke.   The late owner
of the Vyne, Chaloner Chute, in his interesting history of
the property,[1] tells us that it was one of seventy lordships
(fifty-five being in Hampshire) which were given by William
the Conqueror to Hugh de Port.   Chawton was another
of the fifty-five.   Less than two centuries later we find
it in the hands of Robert de St. John (the de Ports
having taken the name of St. John on their intermarriage
with that family), and it is then stated that the rights
of free warren, assize of bread, &c., had been in the
hands of St. John's ancestors 'from all time.'   But there
were many branches of the St. John family, and the
Vyne and Chawton fell into the hands of different offshoots :
the Vyne, in succession, to the families of Cowdray and
Sandys ; Chawton to those of Poynings, Bonville, and
                                                    West.

   [1] *A History of the Vyne in Hampshire*, by Chaloner W. Chute of the Vyne.
Winchester and London, 1888.

West. In the middle of the sixteenth century the Wests first leased and then sold the property to the Knights, this transaction constituting the one sale of the land which has occurred since the Conquest. At the Vyne the single instance in which land and mansion passed by sale occurred in the next century, when the Sandys family, crippled by their losses in the Civil War, found themselves obliged to part with the place, and it became the property of Chaloner Chute, who was Speaker of Richard Cromwell's short parliament. Since these dates the Vyne and Chawton have always been in the hands of Chutes and Knights respectively, though in both cases the name has more than once been assumed with the possession of the lands by female or collateral branches. It is interesting to trace a similarity of fate between two old Hampshire houses, connected as they are by the old friendship and the modern relationship of the families who own them.

We return to Chawton. The Knights seem to have been preparing themselves through many generations for their future position as squires, and to have held land in the parish at any rate since the time of Edward II. It is hardly probable that the St. Johns ever lived in the place, although an ' extent of the Manor ' in 1302 states that it consisted of a ' capital messuage with a garden and other easements of the Court worth 10s.,' as well as about 500 acres of land. In the absence of the great folk it would be easier for a local family to assert itself ; and we find the Knights prominent in the earliest Court Rolls which have been preserved.

In

In 1524 William Knight had a lease of the ' cite of the Manor place ' and farm of Chawton, with the West Park, for which he paid £25. This lease was renewed to ' John Knight the younger,' and afterwards (1551) the land included in it was sold to him.

It was stated above that there has been only one sale of Chawton. This statement requires correction so far as the Manor and Advowson are concerned. These latter rights were sold in 1558 to Thomas Arundel, and his son sold them in turn to Nicholas Knight (son of John) in 1578. The Knights were now fairly fixed in their new possession. Nicholas had a large family, and his eldest son John was in a position to carry on extensive building operations at the Manor House and its stables, his accounts for which are still in existence; nor has the Mansion itself been much changed from the state in which he left it. There are many indications to show that he was building on to an old house—for we know that an older moated house existed, and John Knight took a good deal of trouble to fill up the moat. We shall see later on how far it is possible to distinguish between the portions of the Manor House added by him and those which he found already in existence.

John Knight was evidently a man of some importance. In 1588 he contributed £50 to the funds raised by the Queen in connexion with the Spanish Invasion; in 1609 he was High Sheriff of Hants. But his marriage does not seem to have been a happy one, and his only child (a daughter)

predeceased

STABLES BUILT BY JOHN KNIGHT, 1593

predeceased him. His next brother, Stephen, had sons, the eldest of whom, another John, was looked upon as heir; and the following entries in John Knight's accounts show his care for his nephew: ' To Mr. Knight of Froyle for teaching and boarding John Knight for half a year. For gloves, stockings, shoes, and suit, hose, jerkin and doublett.' ' Mr. Starking for teaching John Knight for five weeks before and after he went to Bighton.' Stephen was a clerk in the Petty Bag Office, and an interesting correspondence between the two brothers is preserved ; some of it, however, too full of family allusions to be intelligible to the modern reader.

The younger John became a lunatic some years after he grew up. He died young and unmarried, and was succeeded by his brother Richard. Richard died in 1641, leaving one little boy, and there was no one to represent the family actively when the Civil War broke out. They seem, however, to have been loyal to the King, for many payments to Basing House are recorded. Richard's son, another Richard, was knighted after the Restoration, and the recumbent marble effigy in the Church bears witness to his importance. But we are now reaching the end of the Knights in direct male descent.

Sir Richard had no children, and devised his estate to the grandson of his aunt Dorothy, who had married Michael Martin of Ensham in Oxfordshire. This grandson, Richard (Martin) Knight, his brother Christopher, and his sister Elizabeth, were all owners in succession, the last

last named for much the longest period. She was also the most prominent figure of the three in our history; for fate directed that she should have the final disposition of the estate.

She married twice; both her husbands were men of station, both were members of parliament for Midhurst, and both had to take the name of Knight. Having no issue by either, she sought for an heir among her collateral kinsmen, and thus she was the last descendant of the original family of Knight who reigned at Chawton. Elizabeth and her first husband, William Woodward, represented between them (on the female side) one branch of the ancient Sussex family of Lewkenors. The Lewkenors had intermarried with the Mays and the Mays with the Brodnaxes of Godmersham Park, near Canterbury. Elizabeth found a successor in her cousin, Thomas Brodnax by birth, who had already changed his name to that of May. He united the properties of Godmersham and Chawton, and, like his predecessors at the latter place, took the name of Knight. It was during his tenure of the property that an important event occurred in the history of the estate and Manor of Chawton, viz. the enclosure of the common land, which was carried out in 1740–1.

Thomas Brodnax's wife was a Monke, her mother was a Stringer, and *her* mother was an Austen, of Broadford Manor, Horsmonden. This lady's great-nephew, George Austen, Rector of Steventon and Deane, was therefore second cousin to Brodnax. Brodnax's son Thomas and his

wife,

wife, Catherine Knatchbull by birth (whose beautiful portraits by Romney now adorn the dining-room at Chawton), were childless, and when they were casting about for a successor their thoughts fell upon George Austen and his family. They were not very near cousins, but George was a man of some mark, and his family seemed likely to do well in the world. So the tradition tells us that an invitation was dispatched from Mr. and Mrs. Knight to the George Austens, asking them to allow their son Edward to spend the summer holidays with them. It is said that the father hesitated for fear of the unsettlement of the boy's work, but that the

BAPTISMAL CERTIFICATE OF JANE AUSTEN

mother (Cassandra Leigh by birth, a woman of great liveliness and acuteness) clinched the matter by saying, ' Let the child go.' The child went, and was eventually adopted by his kind cousins, and became Mr. Knight of Godmersham and Chawton.

The children of George Austen made up a remarkable family. Both of Edward's two clergymen brothers were men of more than usual ability, and two other brothers rose to be admirals : one of them to be Admiral of the

Fleet

Fleet. Of their younger sister, Jane, we need say nothing more than that she *was* Jane Austen; of the elder, Cassandra, we need only say that Jane Austen, like Christina Rossetti, loved to speak of her elder sister as of one wiser than herself.

Among the family a bond of attachment of unusual strength existed. It was an especial pleasure to Edward and his brothers to be able to add to the comforts of their mother and sisters. All of them did this as far as they could; but Edward's desire was as strong as that of the others and his resources were greater. He planted the ladies in a house in Chawton village, which he made comfortable for their reception, and often asked his mother if anything was wanting. Here Mrs. Austen, Cassandra, and Jane lived from 1809 onwards; here the greater part of Jane's books were written, and the whole of them were prepared for publication; and from this house she was taken in May 1817 in the vain hope that her life might be prolonged under the treatment of a Winchester doctor.

Opposite to the house in which the ladies lived at Chawton (the position of which we have already described) is a small pond. This pond gave Jane Austen the opportunity of suggesting to a nephew that perhaps, after an unsuccessful attempt for a scholarship at Oxford, he would be ordered for a change of air to the sea, ' or to a house by the side of a very considerable pond.'

Mrs.

Mrs. Austen continued to reside in 'the Cottage' (as it was always called) until her death in 1827, and Cassandra until hers in 1845.   The Cottage then ceased to be used for family pur-poses ; and with this change in its destination our introductory sketch of the history of Chawton must be brought to an end.

WOOD CARVING FROM HALL SCREEN
(Abraham and Isaac)

C 2

PEDIGREE I.

DE PORTS, ST. JOHNS, ETC.

Hugh de Port.

Henry de Port.

John de Port.

Adam de Port = Mabel de Aureval
                (Heiress of the St. Johns).

William de St. John.

Robert de St. John, *ob.* 1266.

John de St. John, *ob.* 1301.

John de St. John, *ob.* 1329.

Hugh de St. John   =   Mirabel.
    ob. 1337.   She = 2nd Thos. de Aspale.

Edmund   Margaret   = John   Isabella   = Luke
de St. John,   de St. John.   de St. Philibert. de St. John,   Poynings,
ob. 1347.   *ob.* 1361.   *ob.* 1393.   *ob.* 1385.

                            John de St. John   Thomas Poynings,
                                ob. s.p. 1361.   *ob.* 1428.

                                                        Hugh Poynings, *ob.* 1426.

Constance = John Paulet. Alice = 1st John Orrell. Joan = Sir Thos. Bonville,
Poynings   2nd Sir Thos.   *ob.* 1467.
                            Kingestone
                                                    John Bonville,
                                                        nat. 1413,
                                                        ob. 1494.

Anne = Copleston. Florence = Sir Humphrey Elizabeth = Sir Thomas West,
                   nat. 1472, Fulford.   *nat.* 1473.   L. La Warr,
                   ob. 1524.   *ob.* 1554.
                        s.p.   *s.p.*

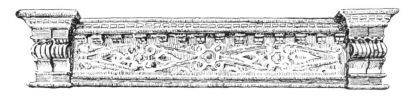

CARVING ON SOUTH STAIRCASE

CHAPTER II

THE MANOR

HAWTON was not altogether out of the world in medieval times. 'The King's Highway' leading to Portsmouth and Gosport went straight through the village; while from another side, in addition to a constant traffic between Winchester and London, the Canterbury Pilgrims on their way from Winchester to Farnham must have crossed the parish. There were two ways of reaching Alton from Winchester, and it is uncertain which was most often used by the pilgrims; but the old name of Pilgrim's Place, and possibly that of Pelham (which may quite easily have reached its present shape by way of false analogy from some word like 'pelerin'), seem to point to the road through Ropley and by Chawton Church and Manor House. By this route they would have joined the King's highway coming up from Portsmouth. Those who kept more to the left would have mounted to the high grass road which skirts the woods of Chawton Park. Possibly this road was avoided because

of

of its danger. When they reached the summit, indeed, a sight of the gallows (which, however, in 1280 had tumbled down) might have reassured them with the thought that they were protected by the law; nor would they have been frightened by the whipping-post which perhaps flanked the gallows. But a little further on the ' Pass of Alton ' might often have shown them how weak that law was. The district of Alton is known to have been for a very long period the resort of robbers, and the ' Passus de Alton,' which was the terror of quiet travellers, has been conjecturally placed in more than one part of this district. There is a spot in the parish of Bentley, and close to the forest of Alice Holt, to which the word ' Pass ' would not be inapplicable ; but it is more probable that the word is used in the sense of road or passage, as ordinarily applied at the present day.

The abode of Adam Gurdon, who was disinherited and outlawed with other adherents of Simon, Earl of Leicester, has been described as a ' woody height in a valley near the road between the town of Alton and the Castle of Farnham.' This region was not disafforested until the end of Henry III's reign, and was a favourite ambush for outlaws, who there awaited the merchants and their train of sumpter horses travelling to or from Winchester. Even in the fourteenth century the warders of the great fair of St. Giles, held in that city, paid five mounted sergeants-at-arms to keep the Pass of Alton during the continuance of the fair, according to custom. In

Langland's

Langland's poem of ' Piers Ploughman,' Peace is described as being robbed on his way to Winchester Fair :

> ' Ye, thorugh the pass of Aultone
> Poverte myght passe
> Withouten peril of robbynge,
> For where poverte may paas,
> Peace followeth after.'

There is a picturesque story of a personal encounter between Adam Gurdon and Prince Edward. The prince, we are told, ' desirous of putting an end to the troubles which had so long harassed the Kingdom, pursued the arch-rebel into his fastnesses ; attacked his camp ; leaped over the entrenchments, and singling out Gurdon, ran him down, wounded him, and took him prisoner. He raised the fallen veteran from the ground, he pardoned him, he admitted him into his confidence, and introduced him to the Queen, then lying at Guildford, that very evening. This unmerited and unexpected lenity melted the heart of the rugged Gurdon at once ; he became in an instant a loyal and useful subject, trusted and employed in matters of moment by Edward when King, and confided in till the day of his death.' [1]

It will be seen that this account places the ' Pass of Alton ' on the Farnham side of the town, but we have authority in favour of the existence of a ' Pass of Alton ' in the Manor of Chawton. In a grant [2] by John de St. John in the 14th of Edward

---

[1] These extracts are from the *History of Alton* by William Curtis (page 19), who quotes various authorities.

[2] For the text of these grants see Appendix I.

Edward II, the land affected is described as extending ' towards Mundchamesrude on the West' and abutting ' on
the highway by the Pass of Aultone on the North.' Again,
in a grant of 17th of Edward II, part of the land is described
as lying ' next Le Paas between the land of the Chaplain of
the Chapel of Chawton and the land of John le Knyght.' In
the next reign [1] one of the parks of Chawton is said to be
next (juxta) to the Pass of Alton.   In 1605 the accounts
of John Knight contain the following item : ' Payd more
to John Trymmer for hedging at Parke agaynst the passe
way uppon the dytche xx*d*.'   An enclosure joining the
old upper road, by Chawton Park, is still called ' Pease-way
Close'; and a continuation of this road in Medstead parish
is known as ' The Pace-way.'   It is difficult to avoid the
conclusion that there was a ' Pass of Alton ' in Chawton
Parish. Perhaps there were two such passes ; or perhaps
the whole of the route through Alton was thus described.
Although it may be quite correct to say that the word
' Pass ' is used in the sense of a ' road or passage,' it is
likely that the depredators would as a matter of fact
use a part of the road where the neighbourhood of a dense
wood made concealment easy ; and such a place is to be
found where the road descends from Chawton Park into
the plain of Alton.

Between the two roads, either of which may have been
traversed by the pilgrims, lay the Common and common fields
of Chawton, measuring over 600 acres.   To the east of the
lower

---

[1] *Inq. p.m.* 1329.

lower road there were no doubt a small moated manor house and a small church.

The principal contemporary indications that we have of the existence of a manor house at this period are (1) the fact that in 1224 the King directed that two oaks from Alice Holt Forest should be delivered to William de St. John towards making a house in his Manor of Chawton, and (2) the mention of a capital messuage (i.e. a manor house and adjoining home farm) in the 'Extent of the Manor' in 1302 quoted below. In any case we shall find, when we come to the records of the sixteenth century and the building of the Manor House as it now stands by John Knight, that there is ample evidence for the existence of an earlier dwelling-house.

The Manor of Chawton is briefly described in Domesday Book; [1] and the following amplified translation will, we think, bring out the meaning of the somewhat elliptical phraseology of the return, and show how the various sentences of the entry are really answers to a set of questions propounded to the jurors for Neatham Hundred. [2]

1. *Who held and who holds the manor?*

Hugo de Port (lord of the barony of Basing) holds Chawton in demesne as parcel of his barony. Oda (de Wincestre) held it formerly of King Edward as an 'alod,' that is by right of inheritance and without paying any rent or service for it.

2. *At*

---

[1] Vol. i. fol. 45b.

[2] For this enlarged paraphrase of the entry in Domesday Book, and for other valuable suggestions on the subjects contained in this chapter, we are indebted to the kindness of Mr. W. J. Corbett, Fellow and Lecturer, King's College, Cambridge.

D

2. *At how many hides is the vill assessed ?*

Chawton was formerly assessed (for county rating pur-
poses) at 10 hides, but King Edward reduced the assessment
for army service (in the fyrd or national militia) and for
danegeld to 4¼ hides.

3. *How many plough teams does the manor require ?*

Eight plough teams are required to till the arable in the
common fields ; the lord has four plough teams in his demesne
and the remainder are found by the tenantry.

4. *How many tenants are there ?*

There are 19 homesteads occupied by villeins (i.e. by
tenants owing weekwork on the lord's demesne) and 8 cotlands
occupied by bordars (i.e. cottagers owing lighter services).
These villeins and bordars have enough livestock between
them to furnish five plough teams.

5. *How many bondmen (servi) are there ?*

There are 6 bondmen attached to the hall, that is unfree
labourers with no land and no livestock, who are regarded
by the law as chattels belonging to the lord.

6. *How much several meadow belongs to the lord's demesne ?*

The lord has 6 acres of hay meadow in severalty.

(N.B.—The tenantry also had common or dole meadows,
     but the jury are not asked to say how much.)

7. *How much are the woodlands worth to the lord annually ?*

The woodlands furnish 50 swine yearly to the lord in
pannage rents.

(N.B.—The tenantry had a customary right to feed swine
     in the woods, on payment to the lord of a fixed
                                                proportion

proportion of the herds sent into the woods as rent for the feeding rights.)

8. *What was and what is the total net annual value of the manor to the lord ?*

T.R.E. (that is in Oda's time), the annual value of the estate to the lord, so far as the jury can estimate it, was 10 lb. of silver. Afterwards, when King William granted it to Hugh, the estate was still worth the same amount. At the present time, however, the value has appreciated and the jury estimate it as worth 12 lb. of silver yearly to Hugh de Port.

(N.B.—As the manor was in hand and not let to farm, the jury only estimate its value, and do not state a fixed rental value, or say whether the silver was to be weighed or counted by tale in silver pennies at 240 to the pound.)

Hugh de Port's son, Henry, was a Baron of the Exchequer under Henry Beauclerc, and he was succeeded in his possession of the property by his son John, who lived at the Vyne[1] and founded and endowed the Chantry Chapel there in the reign of Henry II. John's son Adam having married Mabel, an heiress of the St. John family, their son

DE PORT
Barry of six or and
azure a saltire gules.

William assumed the name of St. John in place of de Port. Camden in his 'Britannia' as translated by Holland (p. 269), thus records this change of name and the subsequent connexion with the Poynings and Powlett families : ' When Adam de Portu

---

[1] See *History of the Vyne.*

D 2

Portu Lord of Basing matched in marriage with the daughter and heire of Roger de Aurevall whose wife was likewise

ST. JOHN
Az. on a chief gu. two mullets or.

daughter and heire to the right noble House of Saint John, William his sonne, to doe honour unto that familie, assumed to him the surname of Saint John and they who lineally descended from him have still reteined the same. But when Edmund Saint John departed out of this world without issue in King Edward the third his time his sister Margaret bettered the state of her husband John Saint Philibert with the possessions of the Lord Saint John ; and when shee was dead without children Isabell the other sister, wife unto Sir Luke Poinings, bare unto him Thomas Lord of Basing, whose neice [1] Constance by his sonne Hugh (unto whom this fell for her child's part of inheritance) was wedded into the familie of the Powlets.' It was therefore from the

S. PHILIBERT
Bendy of six ar. and az.

family of St. John and through that of Poynings that the Powletts became possessors of Basing.

Our Pedigree will give a sufficient account of the successive owners of the St. John estates until the death of Edmund de St. John, mentioned above, brought the male line to an end, and the estates went to Edmund's two sisters. After the marriage of the second sister, Isabel, to Luke Poynings, her husband was summoned to Parliament as

Baron

[1] Granddaughter.

Baron St. John. Isabel died in 1393, leaving a son, Sir Thomas Poynings, styled Lord St. John. On the death of Sir Thomas in 1429 the family was represented by the three daughters of his son Hugh, who had predeceased him. In 1458 the respective sons of these three daughters, viz. John Bonville, John Powlett, and Thomas Kingestone, made a division of the property by Indenture Tripartite. In this division John

POYNINGS
Barry of six or and vert a bendlet gu.

Bonville took (with other manors and lands) the reversion,

BONVILLE
Sable six mullets ar.

after the deaths of Godfrey Hylton and Alianora his wife, widow of Sir Hugh Poynings, of the Manor and advowson of Chawton and the free Chapel there, the patronage of the Priory of Selborne, and all lands in Chawton subject to an annual payment of £3 5s. 10d. out of Chawton to Thomas Kingestone.

We have now brought down the succession of owners to John Bonville, who died in 1494, leaving only daughters. The Manor and advowson of Chawton went in the first instance to the elder of these, Florence, who married (1) Sir Humphrey Fulford and (2) Lord Fitzwarren, and who presented to Chawton Rectory in 1514; on her death the whole of the Bonville possessions passed to her sister Elizabeth

FULFORD
Ar. a chevron gu.

Elizabeth, wife of Lord La Warr, with whom the long list of medieval owners of Chawton comes to an end.

WEST

Ar. a fess dancettée sa.

During this long period, important information respecting the manorial history of Chawton is to be found in abstracts taken from Rolls and Inquisitions of the thirteenth and fourteenth centuries. We have already alluded to one or two of these documents, but they throw such an interesting light on the long ownership of the Manor by the St. John family that it will be worth our while to dwell on them a little longer.

In one of them (dated 1252) we find[1] that free warren was granted to Robert de St. John in his Demesne of Chawton. Assize of Bread & ale and right of gallows pillory and tumbrell were allowed to John de St. John son of the said Robert in 1280. It was then stated that the old gallows & pillory had fallen down, & that the tumbrell was worn out, and that upon it being reported that St. John's ancestors had from all time had these privileges the sheriff was ordered to allow him to replace them.

In the 30th year of Edward I (1302) an Inquisition ' post mortem ' held on the death of John de St. John gives the following particulars[2] :—

'Inquisition taken at Chauton, 10 Kalends of November [30 Edward I, A.D. 1302]. The jury say that the aforesaid
John

[1] *Victoria History of Hampshire*, pp. 497, 498.
[2] The purchasing value of money in the years 1300–1350 may be taken roughly at fifteen times its present value.

John held, on the day he died, the manor of Chauton, of the King in chief, by half a knight's fee. The capital messuage, with the garden and other easements of the court, are worth yearly 10s. There are there four carucates of land, each carucate containing a hundred acres, each acre worth 3d. There are there one hundred acres of wood, each acre worth 2d. There are there four acres of meadow, each acre worth 2s. The pleas and perquisites of courts are worth yearly 6s. 8d. There is there a several pasture, worth yearly 5s. There are there eight free tenants, who render in the whole 28s. 6d., viz. :—Nicholas Dalron, who holds one carucate of land, and renders yearly 6s. 8d., Walter le Portreve, who holds one messuage and half an acre of land and renders yearly 5s., William Pydargent, who holds . . . and renders yearly 1d., Hugh Bine, who holds one messuage and sixteen acres of land and renders yearly six barbed arrow heads worth 3d.[1] Luke atte Hok', who holds one messuage and sixteen acres of land and renders yearly 8s.,[2] Thomas Burewald, who holds one messuage and one acre of land, and renders by the year twelve barbed arrow heads worth 6d., William le Benetfeld, who holds one messuage and one virgate of land and renders yearly 4s., and Geoffrey le Hacker, who holds one messuage and one virgate of land and renders yearly 4s. These tenants owe suit of court twice yearly. There are there seven customary tenants, each holding sixteen acres and rendering yearly . . .(?), and they ought to work in autumn twenty-eight days for the lord's food, value of each work by the day 1d., and

[1] *Sic.*   [2] *Sic.*

and each shall give half a quarter of corn for churchset at the feast of St. Martin, which is worth 2s. There are there five other customary tenants each of whom holds eight acres and renders yearly 2s., and they ought to work in autumn for twenty-four days for the lord's food, value of each work 1d., and each shall give one cock worth 1d., and one hen worth 1½d., at the feast of St. Martin in the name of churchset. There are there four cottagers, each of whom holds one cottage and renders 6d., and each gives one cock and one hen for a church-set. The total value of the manor is £12 14s. 8½d., from which sum there is payable to the chapel[1] within the court of the manor, 52s., by the assignment and gift of Sir (*Domini*) Robert de St. John, for the celebration of divine service there for the souls of himself and his ancestors for ever.'

The total annual value of the Manor, which is here put at less than £15, had been stated to be £20 in an earlier deed—viz., a settlement made by John de St. John in 1275. We may notice also in this Inquisition the mention of a Manor House ('capital messuage') and of a 'Chapel within the Court of the Manor.' Church-set, or -scot (*cyric sceatta*) was not a parochial obligation. It dated from the conversion of England in the seventh century, when mission districts were worked from centres known as 'minsters'; these minsters being maintained by contributions from the freemen of the district. They paid their 'shot,' or (if for any reason exempt) went 'scot' free. By the Laws of King Ine (A.D. 688–726) these dues were to be paid on St. Martin's Day.

An

---

[1] *Sic.*

An inquisition ' ad quod damnum ' in 1329 gives the King's licence to one John atte Watere to hold messuages, etc. which had been granted to him by John de St. John. For the part of this property situated in the Manor of Chawton, the yearly rent mentioned in this deed was *one rose*. In the same year another licence authorizes Thomas de Marays (whose name is possibly a variant of ' Morey ') to retain his position as bailiff itinerant of the said John and his heirs for all their widely extended barony in the counties of Southampton, Sussex, Kent, Hertford, Cambridge, and Warwick.

On the death of Hugh de St. John in 1337 an inquisition was held at Basing, the portion of which relating to Chawton was as follows :—

' *Chauton*.—Also they say that there is at Chauton one chief messuage of which the easement is worth nothing by the year beyond reprises. There are there two gardens, with the curtilage, worth yearly 6*s*. 8*d*. There are there four hundred and sixty-six acres of arable land, worth 3*d*. the acre ; eight acres of meadow, worth yearly with the pasture after the crop, 3*s*. an acre ; twenty acres of pasture worth 8*d*. an acre. There is there a certain park of which the pasture is worth yearly 18*s*., and the pannage, one year with another, is worth 3*s*. 4*d*., and another park of which the pasture is worth yearly, beyond the sustentation of the deer (*ferarum*), 5*s*., and the pannage, when it happens, 6*s*. 8*d*. The rents of assize are worth yearly £6 11*s*. 11*d*., from which there is assigned for making a certain chantry in the chapel built within the manor, 56*s*. 9*d*. Also of rents at Christmas, two

capons

E

capons worth 4*d*., and six cocks and seven hens worth 13 (?), and two hundred and fifteen (?) eggs at Easter, worth 10*d*. Of churchset, 3½ quarters of corn worth 11*s*. 8*d*. The works of the customary tenants are worth yearly 42*s*. Pleas and perquisites of court are worth yearly 13*s*. 3*d*.

'Sum, £19 15*s*. 8*d*.'

Hugh's widow Mirabel afterwards married Thomas de Aspale, and his death in 1350 was the cause of the following Inquisition :—

' *A.D.* 1350.

'Extent of lands and tenements of Thomas de Aspale, made at Winchester . . . 24 Edward III. [A.D. 1350] before Henry St . . ., sheriff. The jurors say that the said Thomas had the manor of Chauton with appurtenances, in which said manor there is a capital messuage of which the easements are worth by the year . . . The rents of the free tenants and services of native tenants are worth 70*s*. There are there six hundred and thirty-two acres of arable land, of which each acre is worth 12*d*. ; sixteen acres of mowable meadow, value of each acre 6*s*. ; a certain pasture called Oxclose, containing sixty acres, value of each acre 18*d*. ; a certain park called the Great Park, containing one thousand acres of pasture, value of each acre 4*d*. ; a certain park called the Little Park, containing one hundred acres of pasture, value of each acre 18*d*. ; two gardens [worth] by the year 60*s*. ; six messuages formerly of the native tenants, worth by the year 15*s*. [? 40*s*.].[1] The pannage of the Little Park aforesaid

is

---

[1] Reading uncertain ; the figures are either ' xv ' or ' xl.'

is worth by the year 40s., and the pannage of the Great Park is worth by the year 60s. The underwood of the Little Park is worth by the year 60s., and that of the Great Park aforesaid is worth by the year 100s. The underwood of the foreign (?) wood is worth by the year 60s. Pleas and perquisites of court, with waifs and strays and views of frankpledge, are worth by the year £7 13s. 4d. Sum of the extent of the said manor, £100 4s. 8d. whereof is paid to Richard le Chamberlain, parker of the parks aforesaid, by the year, for the life of Mirable, wife of the said Thomas, for keeping the said parks, six quarters, four bushels [of corn], he taking by the week one bushel, value of each quarter 4s. ; and for his stipend 10s. yearly, sum of the money reserved . . . and so the value of the manor clear is £98 8s. 6d.'

The most noticeable points in this document are (1) the mention of the ' Great ' and ' Little ' Parks, one containing 1000 acres, the other 100, and (2) the large annual value now assigned to the Manor. The variations in this value during the course of the fourteenth century are quite amazing, and it seems impossible to account for them ; unless it be by the fact that the valuations of this period were often disputed, and sometimes ordered to be made out afresh. Something no doubt is to be attributed to differences of acreage of arable land dealt with in different deeds ; for instance, in 1302 the arable land is said to comprise 400 acres, while in 1350 it is 632. But this does not account for the rapid increase in its value per acre, which rises from 3d. to 12d. It is comparatively easy to account for the subsequent collapse in

land

land value ; for the ' Black Death ' which devastated the country about 1350 was followed by the Peasant Revolt of 1377. At any rate we find that the total annual value of the Manors of Sherborne, Basing, and Chawton in 1357 was £200, and we know from an earlier document that Chawton was reckoned at one-fourth of the whole : yet in 1393 the value of Chawton, instead of being £50, was no more than £11 7s. 6d.

This is all the information we have to give of the Manor of Chawton in medieval times, but from the middle of the sixteenth century onwards the Court Rolls are in existence, and extracts taken from these will enable the reader to learn something of the active life of the village, and of the customs of the Manor.

A Court Baron was held by Edmund Lewkenor, John ffloyd, and Thomas Weme, Clerk, on the Eleventh day of October in the twenty-ninth year of Henry VIII.

To this Court come Johannes Pescod, Thomas Mory, Johannes Bene, Richardus Knyght, ' generosi qui sunt liberi tenentes.'

The names of the Homage were Thomas Mory, Richard Knyght, John Knyght jun., John Baret, William Daw, William Crocher, and Thomas Knyght. It will be seen afterwards that three of these names were borne by important local families.

The Court Rolls of the first and second years of Elizabeth, when the Arundels held the Manor, contain matter concerning the parish (such as names of people and places and old customs) of sufficient interest to justify the following epitome of them.

ROLL THE FIRST

'Court Leet and Baron held the fifteenth day of April, in the First of Elizabeth (1558).

'Nicholas Truelock, John Silvester, John Knyght, Hugh Bean, Edward Wyse, Peter Norton essoign by Thomas Hoker.

'*The Homage.*

John Knyght	John Anisel
Thomas Morey	John Alderslade
William Beane	Robert Heath
Nicholas Morey	Thomas Eston
Thomas Knyght	Thomas Taylor
William Knyght	Ingram Russell
William Daw	James Burges
Thomas Hoker	Robert Naylor.

'William Hunt and others are presented for being inhabitants and not attending but are pardoned by the Lord :

'item they present two sheep were estrays.

'item they present two white sheep were estrays.

'The Widows Crowcher and Bean and Naylor are fined three pence each for keeping ale houses.

'All hedge breakers are to pay twelve pence for every fact.

'All tenants to mend their hedges within ten days, and for every default to pay three shillings and four pence.

'All likewise to take out their sheep out of the Common fields that are to be sown before the usual day, otherwise to incur the like penalty.

'Hugh Bean is fined four pence for cutting bushes on the Common without leave, and, if he commits the like again, Ten shillings.

'All

'All the tenants are to ring their hogs within ten days, or pay three shillings and four pence.

'That John Alderslade who held one Messuage with the appurtenances called Carpenters, and one Croft and eleven acres of land with the appurtenances called Hobandrews, is dead and that a horse as a Herriot was due. To which copyhold Agnes his wife and John his son came into court and laid claim for their lives.

'That John Buckland who held a Messuage and one acre called Castelland is dead and that one sheep as a Herriot is due.

'That Rich'd Lyster a Freeholder who held one close called Arrowcroft is dead and that sixty one pence, or Sixty-one arrows as a Relief is due ; but who is next heir at present they know not, but have fined his next heir three pence for not appearing in Court.

'That Isabella Buckland, widow, and John are fined ten shillings if they repair not their house.

'That no Copyholder shall let to any under tenant without a license.

'That John Bean who paid five shillings and a penny yearly for certain free-lands is dead, and that five shillings and a penny are due for a Relief, and that William his son is of age and next heir—William is commanded to appear at the next Court to show by what title he holds the foresaid lands, to pay his relief and to swear Fealty.

'Affir $\left\{\begin{array}{l}\text{WM. DAW.}\\ \text{JOHN ANISEL.'}\end{array}\right.$

ROLL THE SECOND

'Court Leet & Court Baron held 7th day of April in the second of Elizabeth.

'William Carse essoigns by Wm. Knyght. Wm. Morey & Wm. Osborne by Nic: Morey. Robert Medcroft by Barnard Knyght, John Alderslade by John Amy, Wm. Hunt & Nick: Tryslowe by Henry Knyght. [The list of the Homage then follows.]

'The Homage present that the Butts have been this eight years very much out of repair by the fault and negligence of the inhabitants.

'That John Knyght Sen'r, Wm. Blanchard Jun'r, John Naylor, Bernard Pane, & John Daw be amerced for not appearing in Court.

'That one sheep was Estray.

'That all is well and true.

'That the heir of Rich'd Lyster, Peter Norton Gent, John Knyght of Kingsclere have made a default in not attending but are pardoned.

'That John Knyght a freeholder who paid 19 shillings yearly is dead, and that 19 shillings as a relief is due.

'That Wm. Bean paid his five shillings and one penny according to order in the foregoing roll. That Isabella Buckland, widow, has a License to let for four years one messuage and 14 acres of Land with appurtenances and paid a fine for the same.

'A penalty upon the Homage of twenty shillings if they
do

do not view the Bounds between the freeland & Copyhold of Tho's Morey and tell at the next Court how many acres of Copyhold Land the said Thomas holds.

'The like penalty is put upon all the tenants if they do not sufficiently repair the hedges in Eastfield, Winstreet, Whitdown, North and Southfield before St. George's day next, and keep them so until All Saints' Day following.

'Likewise five shillings if they do not ring their hogs before Easter.

$$\text{' Affir } \begin{cases} \text{Tho's Morey.} \\ \text{Tho's Knyght.'} \end{cases}$$

In these Rolls the name of Bean, which occurs more than once, is the name of a very ancient Chawton family who held land there as far back as 1308 ; in that year, 1st of Edward II. Hugh Byene is mentioned in a Charter as having land in Chawton adjoining le Estfield. The same Hugh Byene is one of the witnesses to a Charter of the 6th of Edward II. In the 14th of Edward II, John de St. John confirms the grant of some land to Hugh Byne. In Edward III's reign Rich'd Hervy of Aulton confirms to Hugh Bene of Chawton the grant of two acres. In a Charter of the 22nd of Richard II, Henry Bene is one of the witnesses, and in the 1st of Edward IV, William Bene. In the 5th of Henry V, Henry Bien and Agnes his wife have a cottage and croft confirmed to them.

The name probably still survives in that of one of the fields near the Winchester road—Bean's Close. A still more important local name was that of Morey, but as the family
remained

remained well known until much more recent times, they will be mentioned later.

Among the chief duties of the Courts were those of drawing up rules and regulations for the proper using of the Common and common fields, taking care that those rules were observed, and inflicting fines for any infringement of them. There do not appear to have been any formal written rules in the early Rolls ; but that rules existed and were in force is shown by the fact that at every Court one tenant or another is presented because he has overstocked the Common and common fields. It is plain from this that there was always a ' stint ' or restriction on the number of sheep and beasts to be turned out ; but what the stint was does not appear till the 32nd of Elizabeth, when it is ordered, ' That whoever should put upon the Common more than 3 sheep for every acre or more Rother Beasts than one for every three acres ' should pay a fine.

The administration, however, and enforcement of the written and unwritten regulations connected with the Common, appear to have been extremely lax during the reign of Elizabeth ; but in the beginning of the next reign the Court woke up again, and formally put down in writing the rules which had always regulated the use of the common land.

This particular Court was held by John Knight (now Lord of the Manor) on 11th April, 3rd of James I (1606). After reciting that, according to the ancient custom of the Manor, every tenant and inhabitant had the right of feeding three sheep for every acre of land which he held in the common fields of the Manor ' at such tyme and tymes as the said fields have

have

F

have not been sowen,' and one ' Rother beaste or Horse
Beaste ' for every three of such acres ; and that within these
last thirty or forty years ' greate parte of the sayd fieldes '
had been enclosed by divers of the said tenants and with
the consent of the lord, which said tenants nevertheless still
kept the same number of cattle upon the common fields as
they did before, to the great prejudice of the tenants whose
ground still lay in common and not enclosed, the jurors,
tenants and inhabitants present proceeded to make regulations
for the good government of the Manor. First of all, they
mutually consented, granted, and agreed that neither they, nor
any of them, nor ' any other whatsoever, that shall hereafter
inhabit dwell or have the use or occupation of any lands or
Tenements within the said Manor, shall keep or have any
greater number of cattle going or feeding in and uppon the
said waste and common fields than according unto the ancient
rate and order.'   They then set out at length what the ancient
rate and order was, and decreed that, ' evrie one that shall
hereafter doe contrary to this order shall forfeyt for evrie
time he shall offend, and do contrary to the same to the Lord
of the said Manor for the tyme being the sum of ten shillings,
the said to be levied by wayc of distress, etc.'

Next followed general regulations for the management of
the Common and common fields.

All gates, hedges, and fences against and belonging to
the common fields were to be repaired within six days after
the first man ' hath begun to sowe in the said fields any corne
or grayne and to be maynteyned according to the discretion
of

of fower men, viz., John Barnard, Laurence Alderslade, Thomas Knight, & Nicholas Moorey, uppon payne of vis. viiid. for everie default.'   The same four men were elected ' vangers or breakers ' of the Common Fields, and were directed yearly to give notice to the tenants, &c., ' when any of the said fields shall be vanged and shall from tyme to tyme present unto the Lord of this Manor all forfeitures committed and done contrary to this order within three months next after the same shall be committed upon payne of xxs. for every default.'

The next order is a self-denying one :—

' We doe agree that if any of us have encroached uppon any of his neighbours' lands in the Common Fields and the same shall soe appear by the vewe, judgment and discretion of any six of the Lord's Tenants then we payne everie man to lay out and amend his encroachments within ten daies after everie such vewe in such sort as the said six Tenants shall appoynte uppon payne of vis. viiid. for everie default.'

Further orders directed that whosoever should ' drive his cattell along Broad Waie after the Corne be sowen there until the fields are all rid of the corn, shall forfeit for everie tyme iiis. ivd.'   That no person should leave behind him in the fields any of his cattle without a keeper.   That no man should take any tenant, without the consent of the lord and parishioners, and that every man should from ' tyme to tyme scoure and amend his watercourses uppon foure daies warninge to be given by any two of the Lord's Tenants, sub pena vis. viiid. toties quoties.'

Six

Six years afterwards, viz. 9th October 1617, further regulations were agreed upon.

' The vangers or breakers of the fields ' were to have power ' to order and appoynte the tyme of rynginge or pegginge of hogge and where they shall be suffered to feed and goe and whosoever shall not, uppon warninge thereof given in the Church, pegge and ringe his hogge sufficientlie shall forfeyte to the Lord ii*d*. for everye hogge that shalbe not sufficientlie ringed & pegged.'

That there should be a common ' sheepe prynte made at the equall charges of the Commoners that have sheepe common within the parish of Chawton before the first daie of May next followinge.' Every one who did not pay his share of the cost of making the ' prynte ' to be fined—the ' prynte ' to be kept by some tenant chosen by the vangers at Easter, and to be imprinted at the expense of the owner on as many sheep as every man might lawfully keep, immediately after the sheep shearing. ' And if any Inhabitant keepe more sheepe prynted than he maye lawfullie doe by the Ancient rates, he shall forfeyt to the Lord of the Manor ii*d*. for everye sheep toties quoties. And for everye sheepe that shalbe there taken unprynted with the same prynte shall forfeite to the Lord iiii*d*. for everye sheepe toties quoties.'

Next the vangers were authorised to order the ' layinge uppe, or freethinge of all the Common Fields as well when the same shall beginn as when the same shalbe layed open uppon publick notice thereof to be given in the Church and that every inhabitant that will not stand to their order therein shall forfeite to the Lord vi*s*. viii*d*. toties quoties.'

Then,

Then, as to turning out pigs on the Common, the vangers had full power and authority to appoint to every man the rateable proportion or number of hogs he might put into the Common to mast there.

The maintenance of parish boundaries, too, was an important part of the duties of the Court. At the same Court we find them presenting that the ' Ancient bounds between the Lordshipps of Chawton and Alton at the end of the lane leadinge from Ackner were sett uppe and bounden by the Ancient men of Chawton, viz. Wm. Moorye the elder, John Alderslade, and Thomas Moorye the elder, and that the holes which were digged about the beginning of October last and filled with stones at and by the Knappe or Green Hill at thend of the said lane, and the bounds at the greene hill or Knappe near Mayden Lane Gate at Robyn Hoode Butts where likewise holes are digged and filled with stones, are the utmost of the bounds by them sett and appoynted in the presence of Richard Dawes, John Barnard, Thomas Buckland, Thomas Pryor, Richard Willys, Richard Mason (clerk), and Laurence Alderslade who were then there and did see and vewed the settinge forth of the said bounds.'

The ' vanngers or frethers ' were to be elected yearly in the Christmas holidays by the lord's tenants, the time of meeting to be given by the outgoing vanngers in Church publicly on Christmas day. If, during their term of office, they should neglect their duties, they were to forfeit to the lord for every such careless neglect xxs.

Although there was assize of bread and ale in this Manor allowed

allowed to John de St. John in 1280, no ale-tasters were appointed at Courts, as was the case in the Manor of Alton Eastbrook ; and in the matter of ale it would have been a dead letter, as no alehouse was permitted in the parish.

The Court of 9th October 1617 agreed 'that if any Inhabitant of the Parish of Chawton shall from this tyme forth keepe any Ale house, victuallinge house taking in and sellinge or buyinge or sellinge forth of their house or within their house to any of the Parish of Chawton or out of the Parish of Chawton any ale or beere, he shall for everye tyme so offendinge forfeit to the Lord of the Manor xxvis. viiid. whereof we of the homage doe entreat that vis. viiid. of everye such payne or forfeit may be distributed amongst the poore of Chawton.'

Gaming and unlawful playing were also kept under control. ' If any Inhabitant of the Parish of Chawton doe from hence-forth keepe in his house any common gaminge or other unlawful playes to the disorderinge of men's servants or any other Inhabitants or Passengers at any unreasonable tymes and seasons he shall forfeit for everye tyme so offendinge iis. vid.'

The stealing of hedgewood or rather the receiving of stolen wood was punished by a fine of a shilling, half of which the lord was entreated to distribute among the poor.

A claim to a right of way through Southfields to Crocklands appears to have been for a long time a cause of dispute. In 1622 Thomas Moorey claimed the right of way, and, after taking the evidence of two old men, the Homage presented that there hath not been nor is any ancient way of right. However,

However, the claims continued to be made ; for, at the Court held 16th April, 14th of Charles II, the Homage presented ' Wm. Fisher for continuing the way in Southfield upon paine of 40s., unless he doe forbear.' The Fishers had succeeded to the Moorey property.

In 1706 the opinion of the Attorney-General, Sir Edward Northey, was taken by Wm. Knight as to whether the above pain could be levied by distress. The opinion was adverse, viz. ' As to the way I am of opinion it is a matter of a private nature with which the Court Leet or Court Baron cannot intermeddle, and therefore no distress can be taken for the pains relating to the way.'

That the relations between the Fishers and the lord of the Manor were somewhat strained at this time is shown by a further point which was referred to Sir Edward Northey at the same time :—

' Wm. Fisher one of the freeholders of the said Manor being upwards of 60 years old refuses to doe his suite and service at the Court Leete for the said Manor tho' he had notice of the Court and been personally required to appear att it, and lives within the said Manor within half a quarter of a mile of the Manor House. Whether a person of that age is exempt from doing his suite and service at the Court Leete, altho' in respect of his strength & Ability he is as capable as one of 30 or 40 years :

' I am of opinion a person of that age, not being disabled by sickness is not excused from doing his suite at the Court Leet & for non appearance he may be amerced by the Jury.

EDW. NORTHEY,

July 22nd, 1706.'

The vangers continued to be appointed until after the Restoration ; the last of such consecutive appointments having been that of Wm. Pratt and Rowland Prowting at the Court held 16th April, 14th of Charles II.   From this time to the 24th October 1705 the Rolls are silent as to the stint of Common and the election of vangers, but in 1705 the usual presentments were revived and the vangers appointed.   At this Court the Homage also present that the stocks and whipping (' wiping ') post are out of repair.   At a previous Court (6th October 1654) they had presented that ' the Lord of this Mannor, uppon lawfull warninge or notice to bee given, att his owne coste & charges ought to repayrs the Pound belonging to this Mannor.'

Bees seem to have been looked upon as estrays, and in 1706 the jury present a swarm of bees found in the Manor of Chawton, ' which Bees are now in the Custody of Mr. Wm. Fisher the younger, and belong to the Lord of the Manor, having no owner appearing.'   At the same Court they present Mr. William Fisher, senior, for not paying a couple of capons for his quit rent due to the lord of this Manor at Christmas.

At the Court held 24th September 1729, by Bulstrode Knight and Elizabeth his wife, the jury present that there shall be four persons chose ' vongers ' of the common fields, to be chosen in the Christmas holidays, and whoever refuses to come to the election shall forfeit to the lord 3s. 4d.   So by this time the ancient name of ' vangers ' for the breakers up and freethers of the common fields had been corrupted into vongers.'

'vongers.' Their duties came altogether to an end on the
enclosure of Common and common fields in 1741.

It seems not improbable that during this period the lord
of the Manor, or possibly some of the larger commoners, had
been buying up the rights of smaller inhabitants ; for when
the Enclosure Bill was passed there were only seven commoners
besides the lord and the rector to receive allotments of land,
and of these seven, two were non-resident corporations. The
number appears insignificant when compared with those
who attended the earlier Courts, and who displayed so much
activity and interest in the life of the parish.

It will interest some to know the names of those summoned
to attend the Court two hundred years ago :—

William Fisher	Edward Harris
Tho's Prior	John Harris
John Dawes	Wm. French
Andrew Eyres	Thomas Oliver
Rob't Boldover	Francis Pink
Rob't Carter	James Pink
John Lipscombe	John Privett
Rowland Prowting	Rob't Jowning
James Mumford	Rich'd Knight
Tho's Eames	Thomas Morley
John Alderslade	Jethro Eames
Henry Strudwick	Tho's Baker
William Woodward	John Naish.
Robert Grover.	

Of this list of names, there is only one still to be found in
Chawton,

Chawton, that of French, though more than one family can trace their descent from Richard Knight on the female side.

From the list the name of one of the principal of the old families of Chawton is absent—that of Morey. As long ago as the 1st year of Henry IV and again in the 5th of Henry V John Moury is witness to a grant of land in Chawton. Probably the Chantry Certificate of Edward VI—which mentions an obit celebrated in the Church for ' Thomas Moore '—refers to a member of this family ; certainly the name occurs among the Homage in each of the early Court Rolls. Possibly 'Thomas Moore' was the same as Thomas Mory, who died in 1503, and bequeathed to the high altar of the Church of Chawton ' for tithes forgotten' 6/8 ; he also directed his son to find a priest in the parish church there to celebrate for one whole year for the souls of himself, his two wives, and various relations, receiviug for his pains £6 13s. 4d. He also directed that a tenement in Alton Eastbrook 'in which William dwells, paying a yearly rent of 6/8, shall serve an annual obit for ever, for my soul and the souls abovesaid'; the obit to be kept every year in the week following Passion Sunday ; and one-half of the 6/8 to go to the poor. Mory also bequeathed 20/- to the parish church of Chawton, and four ewes to the maintenance of 'le Pascall' (the Easter Sepulchre) in the said church.

MOREY
Ermine three bars nebulée sa.

In the eighteenth century Mrs. Elizabeth Knight considered the family of sufficient importance to have a record kept of the

births

births and deaths of several generations, although by that time the male line was extinct. The last representative of the family bearing the name was Thomas Moorey, who, in the words of the inscription on his daughter's monument, ' in the Great Rebellion fighting for Monarchy & Episcopacy against the implacable enemies to both, was unfortunately slain,' leaving a daughter Anne ' scarce a year old.' This Anne married William Fisher in 1660. The only issue of this marriage was a son, William, who married in 1716 Mary, the daughter of William Forbes of Farnham. This lady survived her husband, and married Dr. John Harris of Ashe, dying in 1748. Her

FISHER
Or a fess cotised sa.

only son, Forbes Fisher, died unmarried in 1760, and was succeeded by his sister Mary, the wife of Fairmedow Penyston. It was her son, Francis Penyston, who in 1822 sold the old Morey property to Edward Knight. It comprised, with other land, Wood Barn and Southfield farms, land in the Low Grounds, and the house in the centre of the village on the north side of the highroad. Of this house the greater part was pulled down about 1850, leaving only the offices, which were converted into a small farmhouse. The arms borne by the Moreys were ermine three bars nebulée sable; by the Fishers, or a fess cotised sable.

We must not pass without notice another old Chawton family whose name is to be found in the above list, though it is now extinct—that of Prowting. For upwards of two hundred years the Prowtings were first copyholders and then free-holders in the parish. Rowland Prowting and his son Thomas

were

were admitted to a copyhold in Stonehills, 21st of Charles II, and from that time onwards the family appear to have taken an active part in parochial politics, gradually rising in importance, Wm. Prowting being a Justice of the Peace and Deputy Lieutenant for the county. On his death in 1821 without male issue, the property, of which the house lately called Denmead was the dwelling-house, went to his daughter Ann Mary, wife of Capt. Benjamin Clement, R.N. Of their three children, Benjamin, Anne Mary, and William Thomas, the two former held the property in succession, and after their death without issue it devolved upon the daughter of William Thomas, Lilias Edith Clement. She died unmarried in 1895, and the property was then sold.

The extracts from the Court Rolls which have been given above show an active life in this small village community, and a real desire to do justice between man and man. The lord was no doubt possessed of important rights and privileges, but even he had definite duties to discharge. His land was made up in great part of strips in the open field, and these would be subjected to the same course of tillage as those of his neighbours. Even in his own Court he, or rather his steward, hardly occupied the position of a judge. The tenantry, forming what answered to a jury, were virtually his assessors, and, as we have seen above, do not hesitate to call on him to carry out his obligations by repairing the stocks, whipping-post and pound ; rough and ready methods, no doubt, but probably then considered necessary for ensuring the safety and good order of the community. A different set of ideas is introduced by the edicts against alehouses and indiscriminate gambling.

gambling. Whether these regulations were made at the instance of the lord or tenants does not appear. The date of the later rules (1617) seems to suggest that possibly they may have been dictated by the rising power of Puritanism, but the beginning of the reign of Elizabeth is too early for the influence of this particular movement. If they were really prompted by zeal for temperance, and not in the interests of any private monopoly—and the rules controlling gaming and unlawful playing show that moral interests counted for something in the Courts—they were in advance of their age. In this connexion it may be mentioned that in 1748 a petition was signed by the rector, churchwardens, overseers, and two other parishioners, ' that no Public House may be licenced hereafter for the selling of Beer, Ale, Wine, Brandy, Punch or other Liquors within the said Parish of Chawton.' [1]

The amount of the demesne lands in the Manor was considerable.

A

[1] Some control, however, over the alehouses in the interests of religion and morality was not unusual in Manorial Courts. We may instance a recognisance entered into in the reign of Elizabeth by an intending tenant of an alehouse at Bricet in Suffolk (a Manor belonging to King's College, Cambridge). The condition of this recognisance was that the tenant ' do keepe his saide Alehouse honestlie and lawfullye accordinge to the lawes and Statutes of this Realme ; And also doo not suffer or permyt anye suspicious person or persons vacabondes quarelers or thieves to his knowledge theire to be maynteyned or keapte or lodged And also doo not suffer or mayneteyne anye unlawful games as bowles tennys dyse cardes tables and suche other lyke, there to bee used by anye person or persons Nor keape anye companye in the said howse eatinge drynkynge or playing in the tyme of anye service or sermon in the parysh Church there or at any unlawfull tyme.' In the same way we learn (*The Manor and Manorial Records*, N. J. Hone) that at Gnossall in Staffordshire in the 21st of Elizabeth certain persons were fined for permitting divers unlawful games, called ' le cards ' and ' le Tables ' to be played by divers unknown men in their several houses there, against the form of the Statute 38th of Henry VIII.

A survey exists which was made in John Knight's time, at the end of the sixteenth century, as follows :—

'A survey of Demane Lands belonging to Mr. John Knight.
A Manor House : a Peging (pigeon) House.

		Acres.
Of erable		481
Of pasture		100
Of medowe		49
Of rough heth		55
Of wood ground		485
	Sum is ..	1170

'A survey of such lands belonging to Mr. John Knight as are not of the demane lands.

Of houses	13
of erable	$253\frac{1}{4}$
of pasture	8
of medowe	$7\frac{3}{4}$
of wood land	$5\frac{1}{2}$
upon the Parish Common of Wood ground	125
	$399\frac{1}{2}$

'Summary—

Of houses	15
of erable	734
of pasture	108
of medowe	$56\frac{3}{4}$
of wood ground	$615\frac{1}{2}$
of rough Heth ground	55
Sum of acres =	$1569\frac{1}{4}$'

The Commoners had certain rights in the common fields and also over 321 acres which formed the Common.

The

The boundary of the Common was as follows, beginning at the Lower Road or ' Shrave,' where there was a gate, called the ' Hatch Gate.' It followed the hedge of Hatchgate and Imbook to the top of the hill ; then turned west to the north-west corner of Greenwood Copse, where it turned south again ; outside the copse across Jays Bottom to the Faringdon boundary. Here it turned west, and continued along the parish boundary hedge to the Four Marks, where was another gate. Still keeping to the parish boundary—here against Medstead —it continued in a northerly direction as far as the bank and ditch of Red Hill Cut in Chawton Park, where it turned east, following the boundary bank of Chawton Park as far as the King Tree Gate. Here it turned south across Great Reads by the west side of Read's Copse to the Shrave, thence along the south side of Read's Copse to the Hatch Gate.

The enclosure of all the common land took place in 1740-1, soon after Thomas Brodnax had succeeded to the property under the will of Mrs. Elizabeth Knight. It appears to have been carried out most carefully and systematically. Nine owners of common rights were in existence at the time, viz. Thomas Knight, Lord of the Manor, Mr. Fisher's heirs, Mr. Baker the Rector, the Corporation of Winchester (as Trustees of Peter Symonds' School), Feoffees of the Free Grammar School of John Eggar of Moungomeryes, Robert Eames, Rowland Prowting, Mrs. Prowting, and Michael Harris.

The allotments were as follows [1] : To Thomas Knight, as his

---

[1] For a list of ancient names of fields, taken from Court rolls and old Charters, together with a description of the Common fields, see Appendix II ; for Plans of the Common and Common fields see Appendix IX.

his share of the Common, on consideration of his right and privileges as lord of the Manor, Long eight acre, and Gibbetts Plantation (not then planted), and the herbage of all the highways taken out of the Common ; and in consideration of his rights of common, Bineswood, Drawhole field, Gores, 12 acres by Worthimy Lane and Upper Reads—in all 156 acres ; and of the common fields 143 acres.

To Mr. Fisher's heirs, 32½ acres of the Common, viz. Great Common, Green Common, and part of Jays Bottom, and 38 acres of the common fields.

To the Glebe, of the Common, Parsonage Common ; and 9 acres of the common fields.

To the Trustees of Peter Symonds' School, 58½ acres of the Common, viz. the block of land between Parsonage Common, Gores, and the upper and lower roads, together with 57½ acres of the common fields.

To the Feoffees of Eggar's School, on the Common, Jays Pond Piece, Jays Hanger, and Jays Hill, and about 23 acres in the common fields.

To Robert Eames, Merry Tree Piece and the upper part of Firtree Copse on the Common, and about 18 acres in the common fields.

To Rowland Prowting, part of Long Common and 6½ acres in the common fields.

To Mrs. Joan Prowting, the remainder of Long Common and 6½ acres in the common fields.

To Michael Harris, Tanners Puddock and 5½ acres in the common fields.

Thomas Knight was to have the timber with full liberty

to

to fell, grub up, and carry it away, before the 1st June 1742. A piece not exceeding an acre was to be reserved unenclosed to be used as a chalk pit for manuring the respective allotments, and a pond for watering sheep and cattle. The highways and droveways were laid out at the same time and left unenclosed, very much as they now exist. Northfield Lane was to be, from the Shrave Road to the Pace-Way Road, 20 feet wide. The lower road or Shrave, now the high road to Winchester, was to be not less than 40 feet nor more than 80 feet wide from the north-west corner of Southfield, now called Hatchgate, as far as the south-west corner of Read's Coppice, and 40 feet wide from thence to Buckler's Tigh, and 10 rods wide from Buckler's Tigh to Four Marks Gate. (Buckler's Tigh must be what is now known by the less euphonious name of Lousey Dell.) Worthimy Lane was to be 4 rods wide, with a gate at the parish boundary ; and the road from Four Marks Gate to Red Hill 3 rods, with liberty to Thomas Knight to hang gates (not to be locked) at each end.

Seven arbitrators were appointed by the commoners, under an indenture of agreement, dated 22nd May 1740, viz. :—

> John Barnard, of New Alresford, Esq.
> Benjamin Reynolds, of Fleet, Yeoman.
> Bernard Burningham, of Wield, Yeoman.
> Thomas Stevens, of Wield, Yeoman.
> Thomas Earwaker, of Neatham, Yeoman.
> John Budd, of Trinity in Medstead, Yeoman.
> John Camish, of Medstead, Yeoman.

Their award was confirmed by Act of Parliament in 1740–1.

The expenses of the enclosure amounted to £223 16s. $11\frac{1}{2}d$.

and

H

and were paid by the commoners and the lord of the Manor, rateably in proportion to the number of acres allotted to them.

The items were :—

	£	s.	d.
' Edward Randell's Bill for surveying & making the Common Fields and setting out the several allotments therin, being 309 acres @ 12*d.* per acre	15	9	0
Ditto for the Common, being 321 acres @ 8*d.* p. acre	10	14	0
Mr. Baker's Bill for drawing & engrossing Articles of reference, & the award, & attendance, etc.	4	12	10
Mr. Hamlyn's Bill for charge of passing the act	164	19	6
A fee to the messengers of the House of Commons	1	1	0
Edward Randell's Bill for two journeys to London and Mr. Barnard to attend the Committees of boath Houses	6	9	10½
To the Referees for their trouble	9	9	0
Bills of expenses at the George at Alton at four meetings of the Referees and proprietors of the Lands	11	1	9

£223 16 11½'

It required a levy of 7*s.* 1½*d.* an acre to cover the amount required.

From

From the completion of the enclosure so authorised, all interest in the history of the Manor ceases, although of course formal Courts continued to be held as long as it contained any copyholders. The general history of the Manor since the date of the enclosure has been wholly uneventful. The population of the village has varied but little, and we have no story to tell of migration of workmen, of the rising of labourers against their employers, of rioters or Chartists. Since 1834 allotments have been provided, and the tendency in modern times has been to increase rather than diminish the number of agricultural holdings. In fact, the general character of the place has been what Conservatives would like to call peaceful and contented, while ardent reformers might possibly stigmatise it as sleepy and unprogressive. But even ardent reformers can hardly avoid a preference for the reign of peace and quiet within the circumference of a moderate-sized circle drawn round their own homes.

OLD COPPER JUGS STILL IN USE : THE CENTRE JUG HOLDING
TWO GALLONS

H 2

CHURCH AND HOUSE FROM AN OLD PICTURE

Reproduced from the Victoria History of the Counties of England.

CHAPTER III

HE Church of St. Nicholas stands within the grounds of the Manor House, and is distant from it only about seventy yards. In 1291 it was taxed (under a papal assessment) at £8 13s. 4d. A Church must therefore have existed in the thirteenth century, and the shape of the Chancel of the present building accords with this early date, although no medieval architectural features are now visible. Possibly the dedication was to St. Nicholas and St. Mary; as one of the two pre-Reformation bells which the Church contained was inscribed 'Sancte Nicolai ora pro nobis,' while the other bore the words 'Sancta Maria ora pro nobis.' The latter of these bells is still in use.

Besides the Parish Church and apparently apart from it, there existed the ' free Chappel of St. Laurence,' founded and endowed by Sir Robert de St. John. In 1337 [1] a sum of money is assigned ' for making a certain chantry in the Chapel built

[1] Chap. II, p. 25.

built within the Manor.' In a Patent Roll of about the same date the King grants to Geoffrey Gabriel, chaplain, the free Chapel of Chawton vacant and to him belonging by reason of the minority of the heir of Hugh de St. John, who is in the King's custody. This Gabriel was not Rector of Chawton; but probably the two offices merged as time went on. In 1540 a lease of the Chantry House with land called 'the Rede' was made by Sir Thomas Weme, Clerk, who is described as 'Master or Custos, otherwise called the Chantry Priest of the free Chappel or Chantry of Chawton,' and who was certainly also Rector[1] of the parish; and in a chantry certificate it is stated that the chantry lands have been held by the Rectors as part of their glebe 'bin out of mind.'

The Rectors of this time seem to have made a practice of letting Parsonage and Tithe; early in the reign of Elizabeth, Justinian Lancaster, Rector, let them, first to John, and after his death to Nicholas Knight. Possibly he was specially impecunious, for a year later he acknowledges a debt of £30 10s. due from himself to Nicholas Knight, and then acquits Mr. Knight from payment of his rent for four years in consideration of receiving meat and drink, and four pounds yearly.

Nothing very interesting is to be seen in the earliest existing representation of the Church, viz. a painting of the eighteenth century, taken from the north-west, which is now at Chawton House, and which faces the opening of

this

---

[1] For a list of Rectors see Appendix III.

this chapter. It consists of Nave and Chancel, and it appears from the representation that the Nave had been lengthened at some previous time by the addition of a western portion wider than the more eastern part, an arrangement which necessitated a break in the roof at the junction of the two. Towards the west end was a square belfry with boarded sides above the roof, covered in with a sloping shingle turret ending with a somewhat lofty cross, on which was a weather-cock. On the north side was a closed-in Porch, lighted by a small two-light window over the door.

There were three windows on the north side, viz. a round-headed single-light window in the Chancel, a three-light window east of the Porch, and a window similar to that in the Chancel to the west of the Porch. Another of the same sort was in the west end, and was apparently the result of a legacy bequeathed by William Knight, who died in 1546, for ' Reappeassyng ' a debt owing by him to the Church. The cost does not seem to have exceeded two pounds. The picture shows no signs of any tracery in the windows or doorway ; but that may be owing to the carelessness or want of skill of the artist. It is of course impossible to trust representations of Gothic features in drawings of that period.

So far, however, as a judgment can be formed from the picture which we have attempted to describe, there seems to have been little about the Church worth preserving ; and this is, apparently, what Richard Knight thought, for in his will (1641) he he directed that in the event of his son (afterwards Sir Richard) dying unmarried a new church should be built containing a monument of himself, his brother and sister, father and uncle.

However, Sir Richard did marry, and instead of building a new church left £500 for a monument to himself, which still adorns the Chancel.

At the end of the sixteenth century new ' pues ' had been set up ; and early in the seventeenth had been added a new pulpit, a third bell, and the King's arms.

In 1733 alterations were made in the Church internally. There is a memorandum signed by Jo. Baker, the Rector, to the following effect :—

' This Church was New Pewed and Repaired by Bulstrode Knight Esq., and Elizabeth his wife, and the Parishioners seated by order of a Vestry, which Vestry is signed by the Minister and Churchwardens.'

The arrangement of seats begins as follows :—

' *On the North side*
Mr. Knight's Seat.

On the South Side
Mrs. Fisher's Seat.   ($\frac{2}{3}$ the size of Mr. Knight's).'

These were high square pews, which were converted into three and two pews respectively about 1859.   Eight more pews were allotted on the north side and nine more on the south side ;

MONUMENT OF SIR RICHARD KNIGHT

side ; the men as a rule sitting on the north side and the women on the south.

There was a gallery at the west end. Mrs. Knight seems to have suggested the arrangement for allotting seats, as there is a scheme in her own handwriting which was more or less carried out. At the end of it is a note : ' I would Place to every House one seate for ye man, & one for ye woman. Where they have Increased their Tenements, If ye Pews will not hold them, they must sit in the Gallery.'

The next record of anything being done to the Church was in 1748, when an effort was made to repair it. The circumstances connected with this attempt deserve to be recorded at length.

On the 8th May 1748 the Vestry met and passed the following resolution : ' We, the Parishioners of the said Parish, having taken into consideration the Ruinous condition of the West end of our Church, do find that the Tower wherein three Bells did hang and the timbers which did support the same and part of the Roof are very much out of Repair, and we think the expenses of Repairing it, fit to receive the three Bells again, will be more than the Parishioners are able conveniently to pay ; therefore we are against the three bells being hung up again, and we are of opinion that it will be more convenient and for the Benefit of the Parish that the Church may be repaired in such manner as to receive only one Bell and that the other two should be sold towards defraying the Charge of the said Repaires and that The
Rev.

I

Rev. Mr. Hinton should apply to the Bishop for leave to sell the same.

Tho. Knight [1]
J. Hinton, Rector
John Budd
Wm. Banks
John Baigen
James Bull
Robert Eames
Michael Harrison.'

In pursuance of this resolution Mr. Hinton applied to the Bishop, Benjamin Hoadly (a prelate more conspicuous for friendly good nature than for love of Church order or dignity of worship), and received the following answer :—

' 14th May 1748.

' REV'D SIR,—I am truly of your opinion that three Bells are not necessary, & that one is sufficient for so small a Parish as Chawton. I therefore most readily consent to the request of the Parishioners, that two of them may be disposed of, and the price be applied to the good work of repairing the Church. But I am at a loss whether my Leave given in this manner, in a private letter by myself, will be a Justification in Law for your doing it or whether my License should not be given in my name by my Officer the Commissary of my Court in Southwark in the usual Form of all such Faculties. I should be very sorry to have you put yourselves to the charge

of

---

[1] Thomas (Brodnax) Knight the elder.

of such a Faculty, the fees of which the officers always expect and never remit, and indeed I cannot think that when my private consent has been given in this way merely to prevent more charge to a Parish which can hardly bear the necessary charge of the Repair itself,—I cannot think, I say, that after this anyone either can or will give you any trouble in so good a work for want of a Ceremony which I do not see to be necessary after my allowance of what you desire.

'I am, wishing your Parishioners good success in their undertaking,—Rev'd Sir, Y'r affect'e Br. & Serv't,

'B. WINCHESTER.

'When you see Mr. Knight I beg you to give my very humble service to him.'

This miserable scheme, however, was not to meet with success. It was frustrated by the active opposition of one of the Prowtings, which is described in the following extract from a letter of Mr. Edward Randall, the Steward, to Mr. Knight, dated 24th May of the same year.

'HONOURED SIR,—By this time I hope you and my Mistress & the young Ladys & Master Knight are all arrived safe at Godmersham, and indeed I think it well, for Prowting has made and rais'd such a clamour amongst the mob that there is hardly any passing the Streets. I am told that they called after you as you pass'd thro' Alton to know if you had a Bell in your Coach. I am told he has said you wanted to sell the Bells to put the money in your Pockett. But I have promised

a

a Guinea reward to anyone that will prove he said so. But
after the last Vestry on the 15th he ask'd some to go home
with him, and Michael Harrison (the other churchwarden)
who had signed the order before, and Wheatly who approv'd
of it and would have signed it, immediately sign'd a paper
which Prowting had got ready for them, and Prowting immediately took horse & went to London to the Bishop & com-
plain'd how unwilling the Major part of the Parish was to
comply with your request. But the Bishop did not take the
paper nor read it, as he acquaints Mr. Hinton, (as I suppose
he has already acquainted you), but desires to have the
matter referred to him by the consent of all parties. But
Prowting gives out that you shall not lead him for he is
determined to proceed in his own way, and if you or any
one move for a Faculty from Court he is determined to
put in a Caveat.'

No faculty seems to have been applied for ; at any
rate, none was granted, for the three bells went back to the
Belfry, which appears to have been sufficiently repaired and
strengthened to last another ninety years. 'Well done, old
great-great-grandpa Prowting !' exclaimed one of the last
descendants of that family, when she was told of this
incident.

In April 1838, the year following the institution of the
Rev. Charles B. Knight as Rector, an alteration of the Church
was commenced, some of the details of which are given in the
Rector's journal for that year. The scheme had been on foot

for

for some years before it was executed. In February 1835
Henry Austen—now Perpetual Curate of Bentley—writes
to his nephew, James Edward Austen, to ask if he will
help him in a Church Building Scheme. He adds :
' Edward Knight [his nephew] is also set on building a
new church at Chawton. He thinks that £1600 will be
wanted. Your Uncle K. begins with a Donation of £500 and
your Aunt Cass of £100. This manœuvre has turned my
flank entirely, for I had designs on her and the Rectory for
some stray pounds. But now wish rather that I could give
than receive.'

The whole of the west end of the Church, including the
North Porch, was now pulled down—and, with the exception
of the Porch, was rebuilt on the same foundations. The
timbers of the Belfry were found to be very rotten. A low
brick tower was built at the centre of the west end, through
which was made the only entrance to the Church. All the
new work was of brick, covered over with stucco, with two
very long single-light windows on each side. The walls of the
eastern part of the Nave were left, but two double-light
pointed windows were inserted on each side, and single-light
windows were put into the Chancel, two on the north side,
one on the south, all in the barest Churchwarden Gothic style.

The Chancel had previously been separated from the Nave
by a screen. This was removed, and the Diary says : ' In
taking the plaster off the screen the wall was found covered
all over with paintings, apparently figures of persons, but it
was impossible to make anything out accurately. The Wall
was

was evidently very old, & made of the worst materials, some a sort of moist sandy dirt, enough to make any place damp.'

In the earlier part of the same year considerable alterations were made in the vault under the Chancel. When this was being prepared for the burial of the first Mrs. Edward Knight, it was found to be in a very bad state of repair, not having been used for burial for over a hundred years. There were four coffins in it, that of Mrs. Elizabeth Knight being of the latest date ; she died in, 1737. Two were those of her two husbands, William Woodward and Bulstrode Peachey ; the fourth, that of her brother, Christopher Knight. The vault was merely covered over with a floor of wood on wooden joists over which was about a foot of earth full of roots of trees ; over that was the paving of the Chancel, across which the vault extended, being 13 feet long and 8 feet wide. It was very shallow, so that no one could get in or remain there but on hands and knees. All the timbers were rotten and in a dangerous state. The four coffins were moved, two to one side and two to the other, and, being placed one on the other, were enclosed in a brick wall and arched over. The remaining middle space was deepened three feet and arched over, leaving space for three coffins in a row, and three tiers of coffins. The vault was only used three times after this : in the following May for the burial of Edward Lewkenor, in 1844 for that of Anna-bella Christiana, and in 1845 for that of Edward Brook—all children of Edward Knight.

The Church as altered in 1838 was certainly a very ugly building :

building : it was entirely cased with stucco ; there were no architectural features in the windows ; and the building was even less picturesque and interesting than before it was altered. The old Porch, plain as it was, broke the flatness of the north side, and the little wooden Belfry with its shingle roof was far less objectionable than the squat stuccoed tower which took its place. The destruction of the Chancel screen, too, was an irreparable loss. We can at least say that the work was solidly carried out by Messrs. Dyer of Alton ; and the Church, which had been made quite impervious to weather, was no doubt looked upon at the time as having been greatly improved.

During the next thirty years some attempt was made towards beautifying the interior : the east window was filled with coloured glass of a very simple character, the floor of the Sanctuary was laid with Minton tiles, and one of the windows on the south side was filled with stained glass, the subject being the Good Shepherd, in memory of the Rev. C. B. Knight, who died in 1867.

In the spring of 1871 an alteration of the seats was made, and the old pews put in by Bulstrode and Elizabeth Knight in 1733 were cut down to the height of an ordinary bench. A new heating apparatus was also put in, and proved the cause of a great catastrophe ; for on the morning of the Sunday in March 1871 on which the Church was to be reopened for service, it was found to be in flames, and in a few hours the whole of the Nave, with its contents, except a small number of tablets in the east end of it, was destroyed. Fortunately the fire

was

was subdued before it reached the Chancel, which was
but little injured. There is no doubt that the conflagra-
tion was occasioned by overheating the flue round which
ran an oak dado, recently varnished and therefore very
inflammable.

The work of rebuilding was taken in hand at once, and
Mr. (afterwards Sir Arthur) Blomfield was asked to supply
designs for a new nave (with tower at the south-west corner
of it), north aisle and vestry. The work was again entrusted
to Messrs. Dyer, and on the 20th July 1872 the Church was
reopened by Samuel Wilberforce, Bishop of Winchester.
It is built of rough flints interspersed with red sandstone,
and fitted with Bath stone coigns, and is in the early decorated
style. The tower is eighty feet high with eight crocketed
pinnacles, four large and four small. Just below the battle-
ments are shields in relief, two on each side. Four of them
bear the coats-of-arms of Knight, and of Hardy, Mr. Herbert
Hardy having contributed the greater part of the cost of the
tower as a thank-offering on the birth of his eldest son. On
the other four are : S.W. with a pastoral staff (the initials
of the Bishop of Winchester), a ship, a Pelican in her Piety,
and the Agnus Dei. Nine of the windows are filled with
coloured glass ; the east window (by A. Gibbs) in memory of
Adela, the wife of Edward Knight, who died in 1870 ; the south
Chancel window (by Bell) in memory of Captain Benjamin
Clement and Mary Anne his wife.

The three south windows in the Nave are also memorials :
the first, of the Rev. C. B. Knight, who died in 1867 after
being

being Rector here thirty years ; the second, of Edmund Ernest Charles Wellesley, who died 11th August 1886 ; and the third, of Emily Adeline Hardy, who died in 1877, and Marion her sister, who died in 1875, the window being erected by their sister, Mrs. Montagu Knight. The first and third windows are by Bell.

The west window (by Hardman) was put up by the children of the late owner, Edward Knight (who died in 1879) in memory of their father. The monument of Edward Knight is on the south wall, with an inscription in the following terms :—

To the Memory of

EDWARD KNIGHT

of this place and of Godmersham Park,
Kent—Esq're. Eldest son of Edward Austen Esq.
afterwards Knight & Elizabeth Bridges
his wife, who died Nov'r 5th 1879 aged 85
He was High Sheriff for this county in 1823
A Deputy Lieutenant & Justice of the
Peace for Hampshire and Kent

He married first MARY DOROTHEA daughter

of the Rt. Hon. Sir Edward Knatchbull, Bart.,
of Mersham Hatch Kent, She died
Feb. 22nd. 1838

& secondly ADELA

eldest daughter of John Portal Esq.,
of Freefolk Priors in this County.
She died June 28th, 1870

Make them to be numbered with
Thy Saints in Glory everlasting.[1]

On

---

[1] A full description of all the other monuments in the Church will be found in Appendix IV.

K

On the north side there are two windows by Kempe. One of these is to Marianne Knight, who died in 1896, aged ninety-five, and contains figures of St. Nicholas and St. Swithun, with the following Latin inscription on the glass :—

Mementote in Dn̄o Marianna filia Edwardi Knight de Godmersham in Comitatu Cant et de Chawton armigeri— nat XV^to die Septembris, MDCCCI mort IV^to die mensis Decembris MDCCCXCVI Hanc fenestr̄a nepotes ei posuer̄ut

The other is to Lady Bradford, and contains representations of St. Luke and St. John, with the following inscription :—

We pray you remember in the Lord, ELIZABETH
ADELA wife of Colonel Sir Edward Ridley
Colborne Bradford, K.C.B., K.C.S.I. Daughter
of Edward Knight of this place, Esq., born 13th. Feb.
1841 died May 21st 1896.

Conjugi dilectæ conjux mœrens

Requiem æternam dona ei Dn̄e
et lux perpetua luceat in ēā Amen.

The small window near the Vestry is in memory of two of her children who died as infants in India, Daryl Colborne Bradford and Herbert Lewkenor Bradford. The rood screen was erected in memory of her eldest son, Montagu Edward, who died in 1890.

There

There is a small brass fixed to a panel on the east side of it, with the following inscription :—

We pray you remember in the Lord,

MONTAGU EDWARD BRADFORD

eldest son of Colonel Edward Ridley
Colborne Bradford K.C.B., K.C.S.I.
and of Elizabeth Adela his wife,
who died at Calcutta Aug'st 22nd 1890
aged 23.   In loving
recollection of whom this screen is dedicated.

Grant him O Lord Eternal Rest & let
Light perpetual shine on him.

The arms on the brass are argent on a fesse sable three stags' heads erased, as borne before the grant of arms made at the time of the creation of the baronetcy, 1902.

On the organ screen are two other brasses, recording the names of the two brothers in whose memory the screen was erected, who died in the same year.

We pray you remember in the Lord

WILLIAM BRODNAX KNIGHT

Captain 2nd. Dragoon Guards,
5th son of Edward Knight Esq., of this place
and of Mary Dorothea his wife,
Born Feb'y 3rd 1838, died at Winchester Nov. 4, 1896.
He married in 1863 Louisa Octavia Charlotte daughter
of Courtney Stacey Esq're of Sandling Place, Maidstone.

Grant him O Lord Eternal Rest & let
Light perpetual shine on him.

In

K 2

In the coat-of-arms Knight, Austen and Leigh quarterly are empaled with Stacey : az. on a fesse between three falcons or as many fleurs de lis sa.

> We pray you remember in the Lord,
> HENRY JOHN KNIGHT. Lt. Col. 1st Seaforth
> Highlanders youngest son of Edward Knight Esq.
> of this place and of Adela his wife
> born March 6th 1848 died at Grasse Feb. 27, 1896

> Lord all pitying Jesu Blest
> Grant him Thine Eternal Rest.

On the shield are the arms of Knight, Austen and Leigh quarterly.

The Altar-piece was given in 1899 as a thank-offering for the recovery of Mrs. Montagu Knight from a severe illness in 1895–6. It is in the form of a triptych of carved oak partially gilded. In the centre panel is a picture of the Crucifixion by Agostino Caracci ; the two side panels are filled with figures of the four Latin Fathers—St. Jerome, St. Ambrose, St. Augustine, and St. Gregory. It was designed by G. F. Bodley, as were also the rood screen and organ case and screen.

The Altar candlesticks were presented to Chawton Church in 1867 in memory of Captain Benjamin Clement and his wife, previously mentioned. On the foot of the Altar cross is engraved :—

> Remember we pray you in the Lord GEORGINA
> CASSANDRA, dearly beloved only daughter of the
> Rev'd Charles Edward Knight, Rector
> born 15th. Jan'y 1879 died Mar. 11th. 1898.

The

The next inscription is of a somewhat different nature :—

To the Glory of God
and
In Memory of

ISABELLA BARBARA SHAW STEWART,

who fell asleep
at Chawton House,
on the 4th August, 1883,
Two of the ancient Bells of
This Parish
were erected in the Belfry
and four new Bells were dedicated
to the service of Almighty God.

We have seen how the Church was threatened in 1748 with the loss of two of its bells. The inscription we have just given records the addition of Three new Bells, and the re-casting of one of the pre-Reformation ones. The six bells now bear the following inscriptions :—

1. Sancta Maria ora pro nobis
2. Henry Knight made mee 1621
3. Her children rise up and call her blessed
4. Her husband also and he praiseth her
5. We praise Thee O God
6. O come let us worship.

The Altar plate consists of the following pieces :—

1. A Silver Flagon with lid dated 1641, with this inscription on it : ' Ex dono Ricardi Knight Armigeri de Chawton in Comitatu Southton. Datum Ecclesiæ Parochiali de Chawton prædict. in usum Administrationis Sacramenti cœnæ Domini.' It bears the arms of Knight—vert a bend lozengy or.

2. A

2. A large Paten, with the arms of the donor in the centre, viz. 1st and 4th Knight, 2nd and 3rd az. three chevrons argent for Lewkenor, and on a shield of pretence argent, between three martlets. a chevron sa. for Martin. Round this is engraved : ' The Gift of Mrs. Elizabeth Knight to Chawton Church in Hampshire 1724.'

3. A Chalice with Paten cover dated 1667.

4. A Silver Alms-dish, bearing the following inscription : ' Blessed be the man that provideth for the sick and needy. To the Glory of God & In memory of George Wolfe.   Presented to S. Nicholas Church, Chawton, Cheshire (*sic*) 1883.'

FLAGON GIVEN BY RICHARD KNIGHT

PEDIGREE II.—KNIGHTS

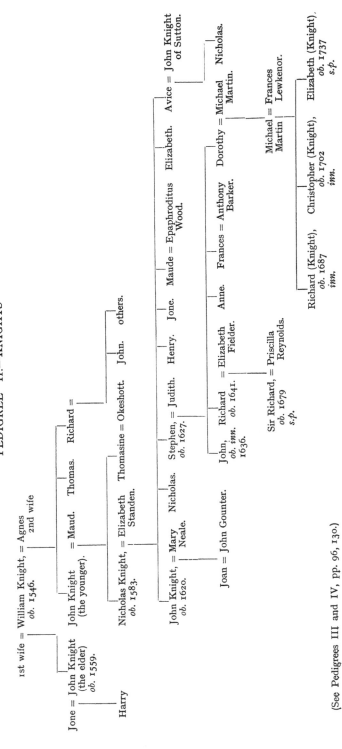

(See Pedigrees III and IV, pp. 96, 130.)

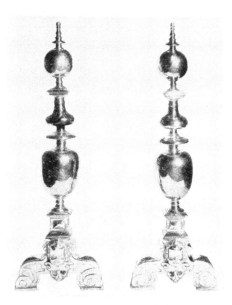

BRASS FIRE DOGS IN GREAT HALL
(Height 3ft. 6in.)

CHAPTER IV

THE KNIGHTS AND THE BUILDING OF CHAWTON HOUSE

E have seen that Domesday Book describes Chawton as having been occupied in the time of Edward the Confessor by Oda. This Oda (though probably an Englishman) heads the list of Hampshire thanes under William the Conqueror ; but the King, though giving him other manors as a compensation, made him surrender Chawton to a Norman follower, Hugh de Port. Hugh de Port seems to have been a man of piety as well as energy, who ended his days as a monk at Winchester. His

descendants

descendants (as we have seen above) held Chawton in direct
male line from father to son for nearly three hundred years ;
and thereafter in the female line until the middle of the
sixteenth century.

That century saw the rise of the Knight family, and the
passing of the estates by purchase.

We have already said that the Knights had for some time
occupied a position of importance in the parish, and that
William Knight had a lease of the ' cite of the Manor Place.'

William Knight's will (which was proved on the 4th of
May 1546) is in the following terms :—

' In the name of God Amen
the xxix^th day of November in the yere of our Lord God
mv^cxlv I William Knyght the elder of Chawton in the Countie
of Southton beyng hoole and perfectte of mynd and reason do
order and make thys my last wyll or testament in forme and
maner folowyng—Fyrst and Princypally I giff and bequethe
my solle to Almyghtty God, to his Mother Saynt Mary, and to
all the blessyd Saynts in heavyn and my Boody to be buryed
in the Church of Chawton aforesayd. Item to the Mother
Church of Winchester iiii^d. Item to the Hyghe Auter in my
Parych Church of Chawton xii^d. Item to the settyng up of a
wyndow in the West end of the sayd Church of Chawton and
in Reappeassyng of xiii iiii^d. y^t I dyd owe to the Church xl^s.
Item to the Paryche Church of Faryndon xii^d. Item to
Thomas Knyght my sone xx^s. Item to R^o Knyght my sone
xx^s. Item to Thomas Locke x^s. Item to Wat^r Sextten of Alton
x^s. Item to every poore householder in Chawton iiii^d. The
rest

INTERIOR OF GREAT HALL

rest of all my goods or detts I giff & bequethe to John Knyght the younger my son which John I order and make executor of this my testament or last wyll.'

The lease granted to William Knight had been for forty-five years ; but soon after his death, viz. in 1548, a fresh lease was granted to his son John [1] (known as John Knight the younger) for the longer term of sixty years.   It soon became evident, however, that he was not content to remain in the position of lessee.   The family were now in a position to buy instead of renting, and Lord La Warr was quite ready to sell ; but the intending purchaser showed a prudent hesitation to complete the transaction, as will be seen by the following letter.   The year in which the letter was written is not stated, but we know from the purchase deed that the transaction was carried through in 1551 :—

' To my Frend John Knyght, fermer of Chawton,   Knyght, I hartely commend me to yowe thanking yowe for yo'r kyndnesse shewed to me.   Yf God send me lyfe I shall deserve hit. And according to y'r desier I have caused my Surveyor to ryde by yowe and converse tochynge the graunte of yo'r ferme in Fee ferme the which as I have shewed yowe I wylnot graunte under ix^{xx} ^{li} beside the Tenements and Copyholds & the patronage of the Benefice but I am content ye shall have with yt the two copieholds that ye have nowe, so that I maye have the monye payed at such dayes as my Surveyer shall show

---

[1] The will of this John Knight is missing ; but in Appendix V will be found (*a*) the will of ' John Knight the elder,' who was perhaps the uncle of his namesake; (*b*) the will of Nicholas Knight, son of John Knight the younger.

show yowe. And I have sent Cottysmore my Serv^{nt} wth hym to brynge me word what answer ye make, for yf ye do not conclude now ther is another that wyll have hit and will gyve xx^{li} more then I aske of yowe. Wherfor I pray send me a playne answer of yor mynd nowe yf ye will have hit and that ye will speke wth Mr. Marvyn the Judge that he walke here in the afterweke to take my knolege, for yt must be done this terme. Wherfor I praye you deferr me no longer yf ye will have hit and to gyve credence to my serv^t as my trust ys in yowe—from Offyngton on the xx daye of Marche.—You^r lovyng frend,

THOMAS LA WARR.'

AUTOGRAPH OF LORD LA WARR

One hundred and eighty pounds does not seem a large sum to pay for what had carried a rent of £25 ; but the transaction was not such a simple affair as this would imply. Two or three years before, the lease to William Knight had been renewed to John at the same rent of £25, but with the additional payment of a fine of £70. Now the purchaser paid for a larger property than had been included in the lease a capital sum of £180, and also continued, by way of annuity, the yearly payment of £25.

This yearly payment came to an end in 1578, when Nicholas Knight, the son of John, purchased the Manor and advowson

from

CHAWTON HOUSE FROM THE SOUTH-WEST

from the representatives of Thomas Arundell, to whom the West family had sold them, paying for these, and for the extinction of the annuity, the sum of £720 ; but this purchase was also subject to the payment of a jointure to the widow of Thomas Arundell.

Nicholas had married in the year 1560 Elizabeth Standen, daughter and heiress of John Standen, of East Lavant in Sussex, yeoman, and on his marriage the ' scyte ' of the Manor was settled on him by his father John.

He had now achieved the position of lord of the Manor, patron of the advowson, and owner of the greater part of the parish. He added to these possessions the Manor of Truncheaunts (in Alton parish) which he bought of Robert and John Gage just before his death. His will shows him to have been possessed also of landed property in Sussex, which must have come to him through his wife. It is the will of a rich man, richer than his parents, who survived him, and who, according to his special instructions, were to be tenderly cared for ; and the will of a man who cared for the education of his sons and daughters, which was to be continued till they were grown up. But he did not long enjoy his advantages, as he died in the prime of life in 1583, leaving a large family.

His son John, the principal builder of the Manor House, as it at present stands, is an important figure in the family history. But what and where was the house in which his father and grandfather had lived ? That a house had long existed is shown by the grant of oak timber from Alice Holt Forest in 1223 to William de St. John towards
                                                              making

making a house in his Manor of Chawton, and in 1524 William Knight obtained a lease of the 'cite' of the Manor Place. This 'cite' must have been a house, for it is stipulated that

AUTOGRAPH OF JOHN KNIGHT

the rent is to be paid at it ; and apparently it was an obligation on the tenant to find for the officers of the Manor, 'man's mete horse mete and loggyng twys in the yere ii nights and one day yerely during the said term,' a stipulation not uncommon, in old leases, such as those granted by Colleges and other Corporations where the landlord was necessarily non-resident, and where the tenant occupied the manor house. That house can hardly have been anywhere else than in the situation which it at present occupies. Both the proximity of the Church, and also the position of the Moat on the side of the house towards the Church (a moat which John Knight took endless trouble to fill up) point to the 'cite' which is still used. But it was to be expected that the new owners, who seem to have been masters of a good deal of ready cash, should undertake the work of enlarging and remodelling the old dwelling. Nicholas hardly lived long enough to begin the work, but his son John made it one of the chief occupations of his life.

We have, however, very little evidence of his activity as a house builder, during the first ten years of his ownership, except

CHIMNEY PIECE OF GREAT HALL

except an iron fire back in the hall with *J.K. 1588* on it. Indeed, during this part of his life he seems to have devoted his building energy chiefly to the completion of the stables, on which the date 1593 is given. From this time onwards a long list of entries in his accounts shows that he was constantly engaged in carrying out alterations and extensions to the Manor House.

Any person looking at that house as it now stands, with the characteristic shape of Elizabethan mansions in his mind, might be tempted to draw the conclusion that it was intended to follow the shape of the letter E, but that little beyond one wing, the central projection, and the connecting line, was built, or at least that nothing else survives.

We fear, however, that this attractive idea must be abandoned; for such a plan could hardly have entered into the thoughts of the pre-Elizabethan designers of the original house, and certainly the completion of such a scheme did not commend itself to John Knight, who enlarged the building only slightly to the South, while his main additions were to the East. A careful examination of the exterior (now rendered possible by the removal of the stucco with which it was covered in 1837) shows a division into two strongly marked types. Of these the older is characterised by 3-foot walls of flint-work and stone, some of the stones indicating by their mouldings that they had been used in an even more ancient edifice, some too showing signs of having been subject to fire; the more recent consists of less substantial walls of the same materials, but faced with brickwork, and adorned with stone coigns.

It

It is natural to connect the latter type with John Knight, and if this inference is correct we shall see that he found a building containing a porch with a tower above it, a hall answering to the present drawing-room, another room at right angles to the hall corresponding to the dining-room, and spaces over each only partially divided and fitted up into bedrooms.

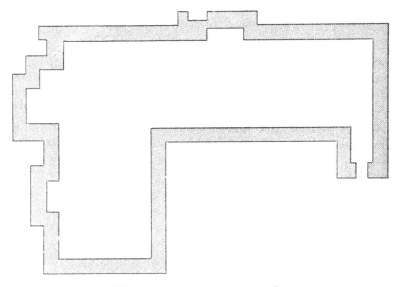

PROBABLE PLAN OF HOUSE IN 1580

The upper floor was no doubt approached by the staircase which still leads up to the Tapestry Gallery, and was evidently protected by a dog-gate at the top of the steps, some of the ironwork of which still survives.   John Knight must also have

found

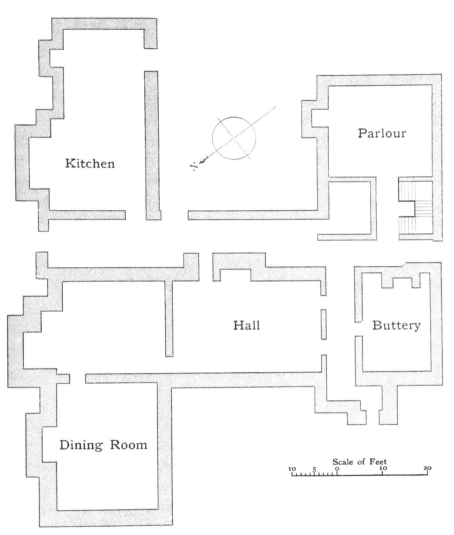

PROBABLE PLAN OF HOUSE IN 1620

M

found and demolished some sort of kitchen ; probably a low building abutting on the E. wall of the Great Hall. The present wood cupboard may possibly mark the position of the kitchen fireplace, as it occupies the basement of a disused chimney, the shaft of which still remains.

His constructive work seems to have included the following : He heightened the porch tower, and indeed all the west front, with a brick parapet above the flint, and extended to the south the main line of building which had previously ended at the porch. This extension, while it provided an additional room, necessitated an alteration in the entrance to the house, as the passage from the old doorway would have led straight into the new room. An excrescence therefore to the height of the first floor was built on the left side of the porch, through which a doorway led into a passage inserted between the screen and the new room. In a line with his southern extension he built a new eastern wing which included the main staircase and the library or parlour (first mentioned in his accounts in 1597) with rooms above. Having also built a new kitchen wing at the north end, he connected that side of the house with his new south-eastern part by a passage on both floors, the upper one obviating the necessity of treating the bedrooms as passages. The bedrooms over the dining-room were probably fitted up by him ; they are called ' new ' in 1614. His new passage from north to south provided space for attics above. The dining-room itself must have been completely altered about the same time. It had a new floor, a new ceiling, wainscoting with pilasters, new windows (besides repairs to the old ' outset ' or oriel window at the upper end of the room which has now disappeared),

and

SOUTH STAIRCASE

and a door to the north, outside of which was a staircase going down to the north of the house.[1] The destination of the great hall (the present drawing-room) had perhaps been left vague. *Now* we hear of the purchase of the ' apparrell of a chimney for the room appointed for a Hall ' (no doubt the existing stone frame of the fireplace) for which 16s. 8d. was paid. A ' study ' and ' armoury ' are also mentioned, but cannot now be identified. A door on the south side of the house led into a fore-court, and it was no doubt on this side that a formal garden with ' squares ' was levelled, on the sloping ground, led up to by a flight of steps. Higher up (probably) than the garden lay the orchard ; there was a great alley below it, and a ' bowlling alley ' within it. There seems, however, to have been another ' old orchard ' against the chancel of the Church, and we hear of one (whether the same as the last, or a third) next to the moat. A gate and paling were set up below, next to the highway, and within this a bridge was built : probably over a stream at the lowest part of the Churchyard which now flows only intermittently. We have seen that the handsome stables which bear the date of 1593 were already standing ; brew-house, milk-house, well-house and pigeon-house are also mentioned.

One constant adjunct of a manor house of that date does not figure in the accounts, viz. a secret chamber or hiding-place ; but perhaps John Knight did not consider this addition necessary, as at least one such was already in existence. When the flagstaff was put up on the roof for the coronation of King Edward

---

[1] This wainscoting, having got into bad repair, was taken down early in the nineteenth century, but the room has since been wainscoted afresh.

Edward VII, a shaft was discovered in the thickness of the wall having an outlet under the tiles. The owner caused himself to be let down into it, and found that it descended in a sloping direction, through a thick wall dividing two rooms, and ended about three feet below the floor of the rooms. Here it widened out like a bottle, and was roomy enough to hold more than one person.

Such was the Manor House after its remodelling by John Knight, as far as we are able to identify it on the evidence before us. It seems to have included all the present house ; excepting of course the billiard-room wing and addition to the offices, which are known to belong to the nineteenth century. On the strength of the date 1655 carved in the wainscot on one internal door, it has been conjectured that considerable additions were made in the middle of the seventeenth century, and, in particular, that the principal staircase, in the south of the house, is of that period. But in 1655, and for twelve or thirteen years before that, the property was owned by a minor, and his guardians were very unlikely to embark upon any ambitious schemes ; while very soon after that date the Jacobean style, in which Chawton is built, yielded to the influence of the French style, which is not represented there. It seems probable, therefore, that the main features of the house as we know it were impressed upon it by more or less continuous operations carried out during the end of the sixteenth and the early years of the seventeenth centuries. These operations seem to have been continued to the close of the builder's life, and the following extract from a letter written to him in 1619

by

by the Rector of the Parish, Richard Mason, shows that they were sometimes attended by a little temporary inconvenience. ' Concerning your intended partition in the Great Chamber, twixt the wainscott Chamber and the Chamber over the Butterie. I have heard my ladie speake y^t shee would wish itt done before shee is to make a bedd to be sett in the next Chamber, y^t is the new wainscott Chamber, of very great value and curious working which is not (after sett up) to bee withoutt very great trouble removed or taken downe, and shee feareth that the knocking in the next roome will force downe much dust and annoiance unto the same.'

Besides the entries which relate to house-building schemes, John Knight's accounts contain items which tell us something of the life of the time, and show how very human, after all, our forefathers were, in spite of their stiff ruffled collars. From the accounts, and from the correspondence exchanged between him and his brother Stephen, who lived in London, a history of his life may be pieced together. He married Mary, the daughter of William Neale, but it appeared that he looked upon her conduct with some suspicion and was not particularly attached to his daughter. The daughter married, however, a man of position—John, son of Sir George Gounter,

NEALE
Ar. a fess gu., in chief two crescents of the 2nd, in base a buglehorn of the last stringed vert.

of Racton near Chichester. She did not live long, for in 1617 we find the son-in-law writing to proclaim her virtues and excuse himself for seeking a successor. ' I having lost,' he he says, ' your daughter which have bin a great greafe to me, by reason she was so loving, so vertius, so honest and so faithful unto me, and nowe she beeing gone, and I having lost a great part of my estate thereby, and beeing left desolate, for want of her companie, and indepted, it hath made mee undertake that which I would not have entered into,' &c. He had, in fact, ' sollicited a young gentelwoman which is woarth a thousand pounds,' besides further prospects.

Whatever might have been his opinion as to the conduct of his wife, John Knight remained on excellent terms with her family. During the building of his house he was constantly staying at the Neales' house at Warnford twelve miles distant, and when Chawton was fit to receive them, Sir Thomas Neale and his wife came there; in December 1603 ' a couple of rabets ' were bought for their dinner. Later on, Sir Francis Neale, and his wife, seem to have occupied the house for some time.

John Knight maintained his position as squire ; he sealed his letters with a coat-of-arms ;[1] he subscribed £50 to the Queen on the Spanish invasion ; he attended musters at

KNIGHT
Vert a bend lozengy or.

Winchester, The Barnet, and Robin Hood Butts ; he assisted in the dispatch of soldiers to Ireland ; he served as High Sheriff in 1609. Later on, however (1616–18), he declined to serve on the Commission of the Peace. We have already mentioned his care for his brother Stephen and Stephen's son John, whom he treated as his heir.

The

[1] For a note on the Knight Arms see Appendix VI.

The accounts of 1618 give a long list of expenses of young John at the age of twelve. Latin dictionary and exercise books, and Ovid's ' Metamorphoses ' figure among the purchases.

The following extracts from letters which passed between the brothers will speak for themselves ; and the occasional allusions, amid the multiplicity of family details, to events of historical importance, will not escape the reader. The letters were all written between 1616 and 1618—they are nearly all dated ' Warnford.'

8th November 1616.—' I have a gowne or 2 in the chest at St. Bartholomew's that are faced with furr. I doubt the mothes have donne them much hurtt, I fynd it so heere in a gowne in the country.'

10th January 1616.—' The imperfection you speak of in your son's speach, I have not at any time observed, butt that in speaking he doth lyspe. I hope he be long since come from you and att Froyle.'

18th February 1616.—' Mr. Nicholas Hyde (as I understand) is our Reader of the Middle Temple this Lent. He is a gentleman that I have reason extraordinarilly to respect, wherefore I praie you goe unto him a daie or two before the beginning of the readinge and deliver my commendations and therewith a brace of good suger loofes as a token of my love and tell him if his readinge had hapened in Summer it should have been a buck.'

In March 1616 there seems to have been a fear lest Stephen should lose his post in the Petty Bag Office, owing to the resignation of the Master. His brother thinks he will find means to keep it, ' and I wish you should doe so, rather than

be

be at libertie and having nothing to do.' He adds : ' I pray you send me the speach that the Kinge last made in the Star chamber against two gentlemen that challenged one another to fight, it is sayed to be in printt.' One can imagine the self-satisfaction of James I over this speech, and his haste to have it published.

Another letter of March contains some interesting intelligence : ' The news heere is thatt the Lord Chancellor hath left his place in the Chancery, and Sir Francis Bacon is Lord Keeper.' This news is supplemented by a letter in April : ' The country newes is, that the newe Lord Chief Justice is lately dead in the West Country, but that the late Lord Chancellor left the seale much against his will the same being commanded and taken from him by the King.'

In May he writes respecting his nephew, and his intention of moving him to a schoolmaster at Basingstoke whom he had heard well spoken of ; but he wishes Stephen to make further inquiries. They were apparently answered satisfactorily, for in the following January he writes : ' Your son was very well on Thursdaie last when I then sent to Basingstoke, the which I did the rather for that his usage at Froyle was not to my liking. Since I last wrote unto you I have heard very well of his new master and Mrs. and doe hope he shall be there very well used.'

He had time to think also about his own costume, for in the same month he writes : ' If Mr. Johnson shall have occasion of coming into this country the next Vacation I would gladly have his helpe to cut shorter a cloake or 2 that I have lying by me which do me noe service, for that they are over long and

and outt of fashion.'　　On 1st May 1618 he proposed to attend the Serjeants at the end of term : ' To bestowe on them a fatt capon for their supper, And I would have Mr. Serjeant Harvye sett his stomake very sharp against that time, and I will then deliver unto him my mind and opinion att large of the partie he wots of.'

On 19th May he returns to the subject : ' I marvayle more that the Serjeant and yourselfe (considering the manner of my writing) did not perceive whatt my mind was of the partie then questioned.　Were he nott a Serjeant and a learned one he should be my cozen Ignoramy, and you Dullman his clarke.'

He then goes on to speak of the supposed intention of Sir Francis Neale to leave Chawton ; which, as he was writing himself from Warnford, looks as if they had exchanged houses. He adds : ' Get for me either for love or money, a piece of very good black satten, as broade and as longe as your hand will serve my turne, itt is to amend a mischance lately happened to a black satten doublett I have.'

On 13th July he writes as follows : ' Brother, I hope you are safely returned from Oxford ; I know I shall not need to putt you in minde of y'r performance of the contents of my former letters.　On Wednesdaie last my Lo: Chiefe Baron dined at Sir Tho: Stewkleys, where among others I was.　Itt pleased his Lo: kindly to salute me, and between jest and ernest (as I conceived) he took excepcions that I did not shine in my country as others did (meaning in Commission of the Peace).　I gave his Lo: some reasons to which he replied nott, but nodded his head and said nothinge more to thatt ; but

shortly

N

shortly after I understood by a friend or two, that he hadd a meaninge to deliver my name to my Lo: Chancellor for thatt purpose. I praie you when time shall serve hearken after itt and use some meanes as heretofore you have done to kepe me from that dignitie.'

In a letter of 9th October 1618, after giving details about a sword and a watch he adds : ' The country news is, thatt Sir Walter Rawleye is executed.'

Two extracts from letters from Stephen to John (written shortly before the death of the latter in February 1620–21) will complete the correspondence between the brothers.

3rd May 1620.—' The King's Attorney, Sir Henry Yelverton, hath lately been questioned about some error committed in passing some grant for the City of London & there hath been speeches that he shall be displaced, & be made but a Punye Judge at the least, but that news beginneth to wax cold again & It is also said that the marriage between the Marquis of Winc: & my lord of Rutland's daughter doth go on & that it will shortly be performed.'

27th December, 1620.—' There is still a great expectation of the great Mounsor from France who is expected at London either tonight or tomorrow. I hear of a proclamation that is come forth concerning such as are talkers of state business and reporters of news : if I can get one I will send him now, if not by the next return. So wishing you all pleasure which these times can afford I rest,' &c.

There is not much more to be said of Stephen, who succeeded on his brother's death, except that he served the office of High Sheriff in 1622 and died in 1627, leaving, by Judith his wife,

a

a family of two sons and three daughters.[1]   For some time
after his death the family was not strongly represented.   His
son John (of whose schooling we have heard) was then barely
of age.   After attaining his majority, and filling his place
as a squire for some years, he became insane, and died in

AUTOGRAPH OF STEPHEN KNIGHT

1636.   On 1st November 1634 James Sessions, Clerk, A.M.,
entered upon the rectory of Chawton, upon the presentation
of King Charles, by reason of the lunacy of John Knight.
John was succeeded in the estate by his brother Richard,
who married in September 1638 Elizabeth, daughter of John
Fielder of Burrow Court, and died in 1641–2, leaving a son
Richard, only two years old.   This absence of a settled headship
in the Knight family during the stirring years which followed

AUTOGRAPH OF RICHARD KNIGHT

may account for their not taking a prominent part in the Civil
War.   They did indeed, as we have seen, show their sympathy
with the King's adherents by making several contributions
towards the support of the besieged garrison of Basing House ;
but John Knight (the builder) would probably have done much
more

[1] Extracts from the wills of John and Stephen Knight will be found in
Appendix VII.

more than this. He might even have taken the field when the
fighting came so near as Alton. It was there that, at the
beginning of 1643, Prince Rupert's horsemen just failed to
catch a party of two hundred troopers ; and, later in the same
year, the town was fortified by the cavaliers and taken by Sir
William Waller's troops, in spite of the gallant defence of the
Church and Churchyard by Colonel Bolles. The movement
of the Parliamentary troops which gradually pushed the
Royalists westward was, in fact, actively proceeding through
this part of the country.

Young Richard's mother Elizabeth managed his property
till 1649, when she married Azariah Husbands of Hocksley Hall,
Essex. We wonder whether she and her boy were looking out
on the 20th of December 1648 when Charles I came by, guarded
by a strong body of troops, on his last sad journey from Hurst
Castle to Windsor.[1] The Council of Officers had ordered his
removal ' in order to the bringing of him speedily to justice,'
and had sent down Harrison on this mission. The night of
the 19th December was spent by Charles at Winchester, 'where
he received a hearty welcome from the Mayor and the citizens';
an expression of loyalty for which they had afterwards to
apologise humbly to the Council. He was taken thence to
Farnham on the next day, and his road must have lain
through Chawton village and onward until, three or four
miles short of Farnham, he descried a fresh party of
horse drawn up to receive him. The officer in command
was Harrison, who had preceded the cavalcade from Hurst
Castle, and whose smart soldierly bearing deluded the un-
fortunate

[1] Gardiner's *History of the Great Civil War*, iii. 547, &c.

fortunate monarch into thinking that he was less hostile than he really proved to be.

The shifting politics of the middle of the seventeenth century are well exemplified in two entries taken from the Chawton churchwardens' accounts : ' 1651. Paid to him that strooke out the King's armes 5s.' ' 1665. Paid to the ringers for ringing when the King came by 1s.'

TOKEN COMMEMORATING THE EXECUTION OF CHARLES I
(Jet and enamel with pearl tear-drop.)

At the Restoration, when Richard was barely of age, his name appears in the list of those selected for the proposed new order of Knights of the Royal Oak. The idea of founding this order was subsequently abandoned by the King, on the ground that it would perpetuate the distinction between Royalists and Roundheads ; but Richard received the honour of knighthood on the 10th of January 1667, soon after his marriage to Priscilla, sole daughter and heiress of Sir Robert Reynolds of Elvetham. If we may go so far as to believe his epitaph, Sir Richard Knight

Knight was a person worth commemorating. Honourable as his position was, he was (according to this authority) fitted for something higher. He had polished his manners, and extended his acquaintance, by a residence abroad, while

AUTOGRAPH OF SIR RICHARD KNIGHT

retaining his love for his native country. Himself a highly cultured man, he was also a patron of artists. In 1679, when he was forty years old, he strove for the parliamentary representation of his county, but died before the election was completed, having been owner for thirty-eight years out of

KNIGHT

Quarterly, 1st and 4th, vert a bend lozengy or ; 2nd and 3rd per chevron ar. and sa. three cinque-foils counterchanged.

the forty of his life. He left no children ; and with him the direct male line of Knights came to an end.[1]

In the chapters which follow we shall endeavour to bring before the reader something of the history, and some of the characteristics, of the families whose descendants, after the date which we have reached, either owned Chawton, or exercised an important influence on its devolution. It should be premised that every successive owner took the name of Knight. The families are as follows :—

(1) The *Martins* of Ensham in Oxfordshire had intermarried with the Knights, and the three next owners—two brothers and a sister—belonged to that family.

(2) A

[1] On the death of Sir Richard Knight an inventory was taken of the contents of the house, which will be found in Appendix VIII.

(2) A daughter of the ancient Sussex house of *Lewkenor* was married to the father of these three owners ; and the third of them, Elizabeth (and her cousin William Woodward whom she married), became the representatives of these Lewkenors, whose property they inherited.

(3) A daughter of the Sussex family of *May*—a family very prominent in the seventeenth century—married a Lewkenor from whom Elizabeth and her husband were descended ; and another of the same stock married Thomas Brodnax of Godmersham near Canterbury, and brought some of the May property into that family.

(4) The *Brodnaxes* were therefore connected, through the Mays, with the Lewkenors, and thus also with their representatives at Chawton.　Mrs. Elizabeth Knight, mentioned above, having no obvious heir, left the property to them.

(5) A daughter of the Kent family of *Austen* was grandmother to the Thomas Brodnax who succeeded to Chawton.　His son, having no issue, selected one of the Austens as his successor.

It will thus be seen that Martins, Brodnaxes, and Austens all in turn became owners of Chawton, while Lewkenors and Mays were not only important links between them, but also left property to the owners.

PEWTER PIECES BELONGING TO SIR RICHARD KNIGHT

PEDIGREE III.—LEWKENORS

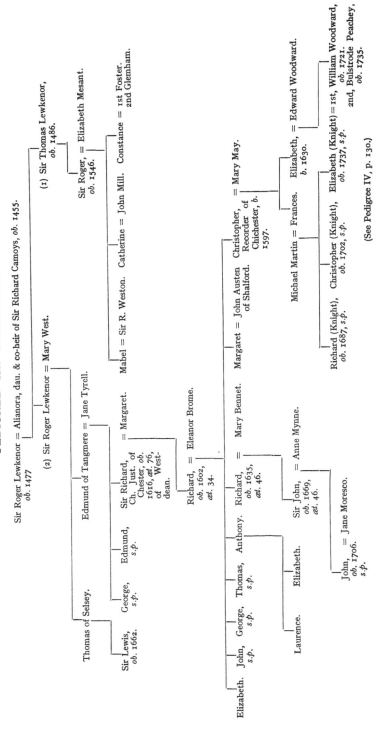

Sir Roger Lewkenor = Alianora, dau. & co-heir of Sir Richard Camoys, *ob.* 1455.
ob. 1477

(1) Sir Thomas Lewkenor,
ob. 1486.

(2) Sir Roger Lewkenor = Mary West.

Sir Roger, = Elizabeth Mesant.
ob. 1546.

Thomas of Selsey.

Edmund of Tangmere = Jane Tyrell.

Mabel = Sir R. Weston.   Catherine = John Mill.   Constance = 1st Foster.
                                                               2nd Glemham.

Sir Lewis,   George,   Edmund,   = Margaret.   Sir Richard,
ob. 1662.   *s.p.*   *s.p.*   Ch. Just. of
                                                       Chester, *ob.*
                                                       1616, *æt.* 76,
                                                       of West-
                                                       dean.

Richard, = Eleanor Brome.
ob. 1602,
æt. 34.

Margaret = John Austen   Christopher, = Mary May.
           of Shalford.   Recorder, of
                            Chichester, *b.*
                            1597.

Mary Bennet.   Richard, =   Michael Martin = Frances.   Elizabeth, = Edward Woodward.
                ob. 1635,   *b.* 1630.
                æt. 46.

Elizabeth.   John,   George,   Thomas,   Anthony.   Sir John,   = Anne Mynne.
              s.p.   *s.p.*   *s.p.*   *ob.* 1669,
                                                         æt. 46.

Laurence.   Elizabeth.   Richard (Knight),   Christopher (Knight),   Elizabeth (Knight) = 1st, William Woodward,
                           ob. 1687, *s.p.*   *ob.* 1702, *s.p.*   *ob.* 1721.
                                                                                              2nd, Bulstrode Peachey,
                                                                                                 ob. 1735.

John, = Jane Moresco.
ob. 1706.
s.p.

Elizabeth (Knight),
ob. 1737, *s.p.*

(See Pedigree IV, p. 130.)

LEWKENOR MONUMENT IN WESTDEAN CHURCH

SIR JOHN LEWKENOR'S ORDER OF THE BATH

CHAPTER V

THE LEWKENORS AND THE MARTINS

HE ancient and honourable family of Lewkenor had long been prominent in the history of Sussex. In the middle ages they had held many important posts under the Crown, had made great marriages, and acquired large landed possessions. The particular branch of the family with which we are concerned descended from Roger, younger son of Sir Roger Lewkenor of Trotton. Sir Roger died in 1477. His great-grandson, Sir Richard, Chief Justice of Chester, who died in 1616 aged seventy-six, settled at Westdean, near Chichester, and built

a

a house which has been incorporated in the modern mansion. The tradition in the family is that the judge did not intend to build this house in the position which it eventually occupied, where the land was held under a Church lease. He had, however, prepared all the materials, and his wife began the construction of the house while he was away on circuit.

LEWKENOR
Az. three chevrons ar.

The monument in Westdean Church, a reproduction of which faces page 97, is a memorial to three generations of Lewkenors. The first, the Chief Justice, who here lies recumbent, outlived his son, another Richard, who kneels at his feet. This son had a large family, and the eldest of these, a third Richard, who kneels behind his father, was (as we are told in a free translation of the Latin inscription on the tomb) 'by the concurrent Love and Affection of Sussex advanced to Great Eminence, when he was made Justice of ye Peace, and one of ye Quorum,' Deputy-Lieutenant, 'and often chosen Member of Parliament.' This Richard was father and grandfather to two John Lewkenors, with the latter of whom the male line of his branch came to an end. His younger brother, Christopher, was Recorder of Chichester, and grandfather of three successive owners of Chawton.

Christopher Lewkenor [1] was a principal actor in the gallant but unsuccessful attempt to hold the city of Chichester for King Charles, against the troops of Sir William Waller, in the winter

[1] At Chawton there are portraits of six Lewkenors of various generations, including the portrait of Christopher Lewkenor which faces this page.

Emery Walker ph sc

winter of 1642. At the beginning of the Civil War, the King's
forces were completely outnumbered in the south-eastern parts
of England; but they endeavoured to hold a few fortified places
in these districts. It appears that Chichester, like Winchester,
had been in the hands of the Parliament at the commencement
of the war, but that both had afterwards opened their gates
to small parties of the King's troops. It was Waller's duty to
re-take the two cities. He succeeded in making himself master
of Winchester on December 13, 1642, and then proceeded to
Chichester. The defenders of that city, though it was, as
Clarendon says, ' incompass'd with a very good old wall ' and
' could hardly have been taken from them,' were weakened by
want of provisions and by the doubtful loyalty of the citizens,
and were obliged to avail themselves of the Royal permission
to make terms with the assailants. The course of events will
be best gathered from the report which was subsequently made
to King Charles, a MS. of which exists at Chawton House.
The Report is as follows :—

' FOR THE KING'S MOST EXC^T MA^{TIE}

' A true declaration made by the Governo^r officers Gentlemen
& other soldiers of ye Citty of Chichester concerning the
besiedginge and yieldinge upp of the said Cittye.

' On Friday night beinge the sixteenth of December wee
received intelligence that the enemy (under Sr. William Waller's
comaund) that night quartered at a place called Havaunt in
Hampshire, beinge seaven miles distant from Chichester with
an intention (as was informed) to meete other forces under the
conduct of Colonell Morley & Sr. Michaell Linesey and so
to beseidge Chichester.

' On

' On the Saturday followinge some of Sr. William Waller's forces advanced to a place foure miles of Chichester called Funtington and there delivered warrants to the constables to provide a great quantity of Oates butter cheese etc against the next night for Sr. William Waller's provision, and that night those forces quartered there and the residue the next day (being Sunday) advanced and were quartered in Funtington, Ashlinge, Racton, Lordington and other places thereabouts the farthest of those places being about six miles distant from Chichester.

' On Munday next about noone, we from the Citty walls discovered Morleys forces marchinge over an eminent hill called Saint Rookes hill in three distinct bodies this hill is about three miles distant from Chichester. Uppon this the Governo^{rs} caused certain gentlemen to issue forth in the nature of scouts to discover of what force the enemy was, how provided with ordnance and ammunition and which way they steered their course. Att the returne of these Gent: they related that Morley's forces (then appearing) were not above 400 men and that they had with them three or foure pieces of ordnance and they inclined their course towards Sir William Waller's quarter. And this night they gave an Alarm. On Tuesday they approached neare the Citty viz within half a mile thereof uppon a place called Broyle heath and in our apprehensions they appeared to bee foure hundred horse.

' Hereuppon Colonell Linsey (uppon advise & with direction) was dispatched with a party of horse and Dragoners to discover (if possible) the certenty of theyr force who observinge there

were

were one thousand horse and Dragoners more (then first appeared) behind a wood growinge uppon on side of the Broyle heath, he made his retraite towards the Citty and beinge pursued by the enemy, after a small skirmish wherein we had a Dragoner taken prisoner and they a horse shott (but what other hurt wee cannot certainly learne) hee with the rest of his company recovered the citty.

' After this the enemy appeared betwixt the citty and the aforenamed wood and from thence lett fly some seaven or eight peeces of ordnance towards the north port of the Citty after the discharge of these peeces, Sr. William Waller sent a trumpeter with a message the effect whereof was this, viz., to lett us know that Sr. William Waller had commission from the Parlam^t to take in the Citty of Chichester and in case wee did not surrender it to beat it downe to the ground, however to spare the effusion of Christian bloud he desired to have a parlie with us.

' To this message the Governo^{rs} answered that since a parly was desired, they should not refuse to admitt of it provided the persons hee sent to treat with them, were such as were not excepted against in or by any of his Maj^{ties} declaraçōns or proclamations and that there might be a cessation of Armes duringe the parlye. The Trumpeter departed and immediately brought word that Sir William Waller was contented to treat uppon those tearmes & resolved to send Sergeant Major Cary and Captain Carr being persons not excepted against by name in any of his Maj^{ts} declaraçōns or proclamaçōns with this further that wee should not send any persons out to them

which

which were declared delinquents by Parlam^t to which we answered that wee should send Colonell Linsey and Lieutenant Colonell Porter neither of them by name being declared delinquents by Parlam^t. Uppon this, within lesse then halfe an hower hostages were exchanged and Sergant Major Cary from Sir William Waller brought us propositions in wrightinge subscribed with his owne name and the name of Capt. Carr and these were the propositions :—

'1. An absolute surrender of the Towne.

'2. A delivery of the Sherife and other delinquents voted in Parliament and all Papists.

'3. For the soldiers they shall freely march without collours or Armes.

'4. For the officers they shall each of them have their swords and one horse and after swearinge not to serve any more against the King & Parlam^t shall have their free liberty.

'These being the propositions wee found some entertainm^t for ye gentlemen that brought them whilst a Counsell of Warr assembled and the propositions severally debated Butt att length wee findinge that in all probability wee were able to hold out eight or nyne dayes within which time we doubted not but to have received reliefe from his Matie (havinge soe long before and by soe many severall Messages humbly begged it) wee all of us unanimously resolved to give this answere followinge vizt.

'The propositions are soe unfitt for Gentlemen of honour and those y^t stand well affected to Kinge and
Parlam^t

Parlam[t] that wee deny them all (except the delivery upp of Papists if there bee any amongst us),

and to this answer the governours subscribed their names.

'Upon returne of this answere the enemy battered us extreamly (they having fourteene pieces of ordnance and by their approaches having gained the East and West suburbs), wee were forced for the preservation of ourselves and the place to fire some of them, which made the enemy for the present retire from the West gate butt havinge gotten the advantage of a Church without the East gate they poured in their small shott soe faste at the East port that there was noe enduringe the walls and hardly the streete for prevention whereof wee placed Musquetires in the garrett of Sir William Morley's house being a place of that height that it commanded the Church soe that that storme begann to bee more quiett.

'Notwithstandinge which the enemy (knowinge their strength of men and our weaknesse that way) with continuall shootinge both of great and small shott and assailinge of us upon all quarters att the same time both day and night for eight days together without intermission they kept us all both officers and other upon duty soe that not havinge men to relieve us we were driven to such extremities for want of rest and sleepe that all daunger givinge way to nature in the hottest of the fight diverse of the souldiers fell fast asleepe upon the walls.

'This caused us again to call a Counsell of warr, at which wee tooke to consideration, what fighting men wee had in the Towne and what store of meate, money and ammunition. And

And findinge a generall defect in all, our provisions beinge not able to maintain us above two dayes att the most (victuall only excepted which by computacōn might have lasted a weeke longer) wee to give time and spare powder (which could no otherwise have beene done butt by a resolution of Armes) wee resolved to send for a parley which on the 26th of December we did at night by a letter directed to Sir William Waller the substance whereof was as followeth, viz².

'That the propositions wee receaved from him at the first parly, that wee did not then nor could wee yett accept of them butt havinge taken into consideration a verball message sent by his trumpeters that the reason why he sent for a parly with us was to spare the effusion of Christian bloud wee havinge the same affections with him in that particuler, for that reason and noe other did now desire a parlie with him desiringe withall that hee would send in two gent: unto us armed with power to treate and conclude in such manner as might put a period to the businesse.

'This message was sent to him by a trumpeter of ours wee must confesse at somewhat an unreasonable time butt wee knowinge our danger in regard wee could neither by faire meanes nor fowle gett any men to bee upon their duties or man the walls were necessited to it.

'To this message of ours Sr. William Waller retourned answere that our trumpeter came at an hower unwarrantable by the laws of Armes and that hee might justly have deteyned him accordinge to the example of some of our party in the like case howsoever hee resolved to keepe himselfe to his own principles

principles and not to seek advantage by such wayes withall letting us know that hee thought if wee had minded the savinge of Christian bloud wee could att first have accepted his propositions and not delayed the businesse to the expense of so many lives notwithstanding if wee had any propositions to make wee might send them and if hee liked them hee would accept of them.

' This answere was soe high and our present condition soe low that we were driven to the greatest streight could bee imagined yett wee resolved to expect with patience what the issue of that night's work would prove.

' The enemy presently played uppon us with all manner of shott and in all quarters as before and in the morninge they fired a heap of faggots at the West porte and hung a petarr upon the gate with an intention to have fired the gate or forced it open but wee with some labour quenched the fier & not without some hazard beate them from that designe. But beinge in this sad condition that wee could not expect other than the losse of our lives and ruine to all in the citty that stood well affected to his Maties service and both without the least advantage to his Matie wee againe resolved to sound a parly on purpose to gaine time to receave succors or to understand his Ma^{ts} further pleasure and accordingly wee sent a Trumpeter to Sr. William Waller with a letter to this effect. That wee had now considered of propositions which wee would have sent by the trumpeter had not his quality dispromised that satisfaction which to every particuler wee should endeavour to contribute and therefore wee did desire to have two hostages

of

P

of equal qualitye to Sr. William Bellenden and Capt. Wolfe (whom wee intended to send out unto them) returned unto us. During this treaty accordinge to our expectation wee received a letter from his Matie intimating that wee could not expect succor till 15 dayes and givinge leave to make the best conditions wee could in case wee could not holde out till reliefe might come : which though we well knew wee could not yett wee resolved our propositions should be such as should not give the enemy the least ground of knowinge the necessities we were under.

'The trumpeter that was despatched immediately brought this answere unto us from Sr. William Waller in writinge :

'GENTLEMEN,—According to your desier I have agreed to send two gent: in exchange for Sr. William Bellenden & Captaine Wolfe our hostages shalbee Sr. Michaell Linesey and cap^t Boswell. I shall expect to receave your propositions and that those gentlemen shall come armed with a power to treate & conclude and by them we will retourne our finall resolution our hostages shalbee accompanied with the same number of men as formerly wee expect yours in the like manner—I have noe more to add butt that I am your servant,

WILLIAM WALLER.

'Accordingly hostages were exchanged and our propositions sent the very words whereof were as followeth :—

'1. That it shalbee lawful and permitted to the Governour, officers, gents and soldiers which are now residinge in the Citty of Chichester to march thence with their horses, armes bagge and baggadge drums beatinge match

match in cocke bullett in mouth and Colours flyinge to any part of his Maties Army without plunderinge or other injury.

' 2. If any officer souldier gent: or other person now residing in this Citty or which at any time within the space of one month last past hath resided in this Citty shalbee minded to repayre to his habitation or place of dwellinge (wheresoever the same is) that hee or they shalbee permitted soe to doe and there to remayne without any injurye to bee offered to his person or estate.

' 3. That if any inhabitant of this Citty shall resolve to remayne here that hee bee permitted soe to doe without injury to his person or estate or if hee shall march with our forces yett his estate to remayne in security.

' 4. That noe man now residinge here and hath done any act for the maintenance of this Citty on the behalf of the Kings Majestie or hath used any words to that purpose shalbee questioned therefore.

' 5. That we may first march out of one port before your forces enter any parte of the Citty & when your forces enter that it shall not bee at the same port wee march out.

' 6. That wee have a Trumpeter of yours furnished with a duplicate of these articles of treaty to march with us, with a safe conduct to the Kings Garrison at Readinge.

' These were our publique propositions but we armed Sir William Bellenden & Captaine Wolfe to conclude on any other such tearmes as they in their judgments should think

fit

fit and more particularly the high Sherife & Mr. Lewkenor
being the only persons sought after as was conceaved did
voluntarily authorize Sir William Bellenden & Captaine Wolfe
to deliver them upp prisoners in case their sufferings might
preserve to his Majestie such a considerable number of souldiers
as might otherwise bee in danger to be lost to his Majestie's
disservice. Butt it seems that all our propositions were sett
on side nor could our Gentlemen get them to treat on any
other save only free quarter and a cessation of armes during
the treaty, which the Gentlemen thought to bee soe meane
conditions that they departed without drawing to any conclusion att all. This being signified unto us by Sir William
Bellenden and Captaine Wolfe we were more than ordinarily
sensible that the enemy had certaine intelligence of our indi-
gencies and therefore wee called a counsell of warr once more
to advise what course was fitt to be steered for the best service
of his Majestie, where two questions were moved the first to
attempt the making of our passage through them, the second
to accept of the enemys propositions since now we were out
of hope of better—the first was wholly declined by the counsell
of warr as impossible for soe small a number as we were to
breake through about two thousand horse and Dragoners
and one thousand foote of the enemy's especially they having
soe blocked up and entrenched all the wayes that there was
noe passage for horse without an undoubted daunger of ruine
by their force and ordnance. The second question was
unanimously harkened unto and there uppon it was resolved
that we should forthwith despatch a messenger with a
                                                    Trumpeter

Trumpeter (though it was late at night) to Sir William Waller, butt first by a commander of his lying in the East suburbs wee desired to know (regards of his former exception to the unreasonableness of the time) whether such a messenger might bee admitted at that time of night yes or noe. Sir William retourned that hee was contented to admitt of a treaty (though late at night) whereuppon wee despatched Captaine Leeds with a Trumpeter with him, & by the Cap^{tn} lett Sir William know that we were contented with the first propositions made by him to us and resolved to quitt the Citty uppon those tearmes. To this Sir William Waller returned by Captn Leeds this answer in wrighting viz^y. To those propositions and demaunds made by the Governor and Gentlemen in Chichester my answer is, That quarter shallbee given to all officers, souldiers gentlemen and other inhabitants in that Citty and free passage out of the towne shalbe granted to all Ladyes & Gentlewomen for their owne persons and I doe promise unto all both men and weomen civill and faire usuage. That the Citty shalbee absolutely surrendered into my hands by toomorrow (being Wensday the 28th of December) by nyne of the clock in the morninge with all armes ammunition and furniture of warr and colours undefaced, WILLIAM WALLER.

' To which was added this post script. I desier an absolute answere within an hower in the meane time I graunt a cessation of Arms.

' Though it were hard to requier answere within an houer (especially it being then past one of the clock in the morninge, when it was impossible to have common advice of all the officers)

officers) yett the governors of the towne with the assent of such
commanders as could be drawne togeather, foreseeing the
destruction of themselves and all other of his Majestie's
good subjects within that Citty in case they embraced not
the conditions offered resolved to render the Towne uppon
those tearmes last mentioned, only they differed from Sir
William Waller's demands in poynt of time promising to
deliver it upp by two of the clock in the afternoone,
and thus much the governor signified in wrightinge by a
Trumpeter to Sir William Waller. The next morning being
Wensday the 28th of December the Governors meetinge diverse
of the Scotish and other officers acquainted them with the
proceedings of the night last past with which many of the
Scotts seemed to bee much displeased for that the conditions
were noe better and resolved (as they said) rather to adventure
their lives than embrace the conditions and in prosecution of
this resolution divers of them mounted on horseback and putt
themselves in order at the Northport to resist the enemy in
case they should approach that port. Mr. Lewkenor one of
the Governors seeing the discontent of the Scottish officers
came unto them and demanded if they would be content he
would signifie their resolutions to Sir William Waller who
desired it might be so, which (togeather with some words cast
out by the common souldiers of the enemy's who lay under the
wall of the Citty & had free discourse with the towne souldiers)
caused Mr. Lewkenor to direct a letter to Sir William Waller
to this effect that notwithstandinge conditions agreed on
the common souldiers of his declared publiquely they would
kill

kill Mr. Lewkenor & seaven others (whom they named not). That the Scotts officers dislike the conditions of bare quarter only, and rather resolved to dye then embrace them.

' To this letter Sir William Waller returns this answer within half an houer or thereabouts.

' GENT^N,—I cannot butt marvaile very much to meete with new exceptions after capitulation agreed ; for any threatinge speeches uttered by any against your owne person or any other, I should desire you to rest confidently uppon my faith that none shall touch one hair of your heads but he shall take my life into the bargaine. Those officers & Gentlemen of my Lord of Crawford's troupe must either submitt to the condition of yeeldinge uppon quarter or if they have a minde to put their lives uppon a cast at dice stand the issue of warr without hope of mercy. I expect a punctual performance of the agreement and that immediately and upon that condition I subscribe myself your servant, WILLIAM WALLER.

' This answer being received by the Governors they immediately acquainted the Scottish officers with the contents thereof desiring them to grow to some such settled resolution as might best conduce to his Majestie's service, their owne honor and safeties, giving them assurance to undergoe any hazard with them. But at last they (being equally sensible with the Governors of ye weakness of the towne, the inability of some & indisposition of most of the soldiers to fight, of the want of ammunition shortnesse of victual and the great disproportion that was in number betweene the enemy's forces and ours) resolved unanimously to surrender the town uppon

bare

bare quarter—which being signified to Sir William Waller he forthwith writeth to the Governors as followeth.

'GENT^N,—Wee are now in the name of God agreed in the next place for your preservations I desier your ports may bee cleared & wee ready to take possession by twelve of the clock at noon that soe the approach of night may not tempt our troupers to disorder before wee be actually settled. I requier six hostages for performance of your covenants viz., Mr. Lewkenor, Colonel Shelley, Sir William Bellenden, Mr. Edward Ford, Colonel Linsey, Serjant Major Dawson. I will send into the town some commissioners to see things acted with expedition.—I rest your humble servant, WILLIAM WALLER.

FACSIMILE OF SIR WILLIAM WALLER'S LETTER

'In

' In the post script of this letter he thus writeth.   Appoint which port you mean to cleare first and I shall send a guard of horse thither to convoy your hostages unto me.

Chris. Lewkenor.   I. Lyndsay.

W. Bellenden.   Edw'd Porter.   Major Lermonth.

Edw'd Forde.   Ja. Sterling.   Jo. Weston.

Thos. Leedes.   Frances Lyndsay.'

The following message from the King had been received during the siege :—

' Right trusty & right welbeloved & trusty & welbeloved wee greet you well wee have had the relation of ye present state of our Citty of Chichester by your expresse messenger sent to us from you.   Wee take your cares & brave resolutions in exceedinge goodpart for the defence & preservation of yourselves & of that place.   Wee are sorry that for the present wee are not able to supply you with those forces which wee acknowledge are very requisite to be sent not only for your sakes whose honour & safeties wee are tender of but also for your owne service sake.   The preservation of our owne person & the body of oure army in this place near unto us, doe put such a necessity uppon us that without hazard of all wee cannot divide these oure forces into parts, which being united as now they are are sufficient for our defence.   Butt wee have at present assurance of supplies from other several parts to a very considerable number and then wee shalbee able to give that assistance from hence which wee are as willing to send unto you as you can be to aske and we hope that a few (that

is

1. LEWKENOR	6. BARDOLFE	11. MOYNE
2. DALINGRIGE	7. GOURNAY	12. DOYLEY
3. TREGOZ	8. ECHINGHAM	13. BRUSE
4. CULPEPER	9. GROMSTED	14. GORING
5. CAMOYS	10. AUDLEY & TUCHET	15. POYNINGS

ARMS OF SIR CHRISTOPHER LEWKENOR IMPALING MAY ON TURTLE SHIELD
(3ft. 6in. by 2ft. 8in.)

is to say fifteen) dayes at most will bringe this to passe. In the meantime wee hope well that by the strength yee already have and by the providence you use in managing your affairs yee wilbee able to hold out as long as they wilbee able to continue the siege in this winter season, which will be for your honour & much conduce to our service. Butt if yee shalbee putt to any such distresse as y^t yee cannot endure long and that this should happen before Our supplyes can come unto you (which we hope shall not bee, wee purposing to use all possible speede in our despatches) wee shall not take it amisse from you if you use that meane for your owne safeties by way of Capitulation on the behalf of yourselves and of Our good subjects in the Towne as in your wisdoms accordinge to the course of souldiers in the like cases yee can agree upon with the adverse party And this wee assure you and those Gentlemen whoe assist you that wee doe & shall thankfully esteeme of these your endeavours whatsoever the sucesse shall prove (which is only in the hands of God) & study ye ways to make you reparations by any thinge in our power. Given at Our Court at Oxford the 24th of December 1642.'

Christopher Lewkenor had married in 1629 Mary, who was daughter of John May of Rawmere, but who was then a widow. A curious family tradition is connected with this marriage. It seems that the lady was unwilling, although two of her brothers were intimate friends of Lewkenor and anxious for the match. Lewkenor had no fortune and was in debt, but was likely to rise in his profession. The brothers, knowing

that

that their sister was apt to listen to gipsies who went about on pretence of telling fortunes, employed a company of them to go to her in favour of Mr. Lewkenor, and placed themselves behind a hedge at the time when she was feeding her fowls. Observing that she let go her apron and the corn fell to the ground, they concluded from this that their story must have made some impression : therefore they desired their friend to try his success once more, when she accepted of his proposal. When married she told him she had a thousand pounds she was desirous to place out on good security. He accordingly took it to London, and paid all his debts, and brought her the discharges.

Shortly after the siege of Chichester Christopher Lewkenor received from the King the honour of knighthood. But his exertions and adventures in the Royal cause were by no means at an end.

In 1646 he assisted Sir Edmund Fortescue in the defence of Fort Charles in Devonshire. The garrison here seem to have been able to make a much more obstinate resistance than was possible at Chichester. They were forced indeed to capitulate, but the articles of surrender to Colonel Ralph Weldon show that they marched out with all the honours of war, with their standards flying, and their troopers allowed to fire three volleys before they surrendered their arms. Fortescue and Lewkenor kept their own arms and had liberty to reside at Fallapitt (the Fortescues' place) ' or elsewhere in this country ' for three months, and thereafter, if they were unable to make their peace with the Parliament, to pass beyond the seas.

In

In 1650 Charles II gave to Lewkenor a safe conduct (the original of which is preserved at Chawton) to proceed to Belgium on the King's business.

On the Restoration his two daughters, Frances and Elizabeth,[1] had each of them a portion of £1000 from the Crown. Christopher's nephew John (son of his elder brother, Richard) was also knighted and added largely to the family estates by marrying Ann, the daughter of George Mynne.

In spite of the traditional loyalty of the family, Sir John's son, another John, was evidently placed in a difficult position by the extraordinary conduct of James II in 1687–8. A letter is extant addressed to him by Lord Montagu of Cowdray, the Lord Lieutenant, containing the following questions required by the King to be put to all the Deputy Lieutenants and Justices of the Peace within the county :—

'1. In case he shall be chosen a Knight of ye Shire or Burgesse of a Towne when the King shall think fitt to call a Parliament whether he will be for taking off ye penall Laws & Tests.

'2. Whether he will assist & contribute to ye ellection of such members as shall be for taking off the penall lawes & Tests.

'3. Whether he will support the King's declaration for liberty of conscience by living freindly with those of all perswasions as subjects of ye same prince, as good christians ought to doe.'

John

---

[1] These two ladies, it will be seen below, were the mothers, respectively of Mrs. Elizabeth (Martin) Knight of Chawton and William (Woodward) Knight, her husband.

John Lewkenor, Esquire, answers to the two first questions that he shall consent readily to the abrogating the 'penall lawes and tests,' provided that the Church of England may be secured by Act of Parliament in her legal rights and possessions. And as to the third question, he wholly consents.

With these keen Church of England feelings, he must already have looked with suspicion on the conduct of the King towards the Fellows of Magdalen College, which has been so graphically described by Macaulay, and of which John Lewkenor received a private account from Oxford. More than one account of the extraordinary interview between the King and the Fellows has already been published in ' Magdalen College and James II,' by Rev. J. Bloxam, D.D. (Oxford Historical Society, No. 6) ; and as the interview was attended by a shorthand writer, the accounts agree very closely. It may be interesting, however, to read an independent recital. The letter is as follows :—

' SIR,—I must confess It's something above a week since I received y^r last letter, & that I did not answer it sooner I have but little to say for my excuse if I consider what vast encouragement of matter for a letter ye present Juncture of affairs has afforded : only this, wth y^r leave let me implead that I could not but think that most of w^t happened was of such publick concern that you could not fail of a particular account of it in y^r publick letters, but however this could not I was convinced excuse me from my duty of serving you in w^t lay in my power and that a tautology in a few words was

much

much more tolerable than a Soloecism in good manners. I have therefore ventured to send you this impartiall account of ye Magdalen business as 'twas taken from King's mouth in shorthand which I do not find in any publick letters. The Lord Sunderland sent an order to ye Fellows of Magd: Coll. that they should attend ye K: at three of the clock in ye afternoon on Sunday. They waited on His Maj^ty accordingly & Dr. Pudsey ye Senr Fellow was to answer whatever His Maj^ty requir'd of y^m.

' As soon as they were admitted His Maj: began as follows.

K. What's your name ?   Dr Pudsey ?

Dr. P. Yes may it please yr Majesty.

K. Did you receive my letter ?

Dr. P. Yes, S^r, Wee did.

K. Then you have not dealt wth me like Gentlemen : you have done very uncivilly & undutifully by me.   Upon which they all kneel'd & Dr Pudsey offer'd a Peticõn containing the reasons & obligations they had to proceed as they did, wch His Maj: refus'd to take & said on.

K. You have been a stubborn turbulent College. I have known you to be so these 26 years myself : you have affronted me : Is this your Ch: England's Loyalty ? One would wonder to see so many Ch: of Eng: men got together in such a business.   Go back & shew yourselves good members of y^r Ch: of Eng^d, Get you gone. Know I am y^r King & y^t I command you to be gone.   Goe & admitt ye Bishop of Oxford Head Principall (or wh^t do you call it) of y^r Coll: (one that stood by said " President ")

I

I mean President of y^r Coll Lett them that refuse look to it. You shall feel the weight of y^r Sovereign's displeasure. The Fellows being gone out of ye Dean's Lodgings were called back and ye King said

K. I hear you have admitted a fellow of y^r Coll since you receiv'd my Inhibition, is this true ?   Hav't you admitted one Mr. Holding fellow ?

Dr. P. I think he was admitted, but we conceive—— (the doctor hesitates a little) another of the Fellows said, May it please y^r Majesty, there was no election, or admission since your Maj^{tys} Inhibition ; but only the Confirmation of ye former Election.

K. The confirmation of a former Election 'twas downright disobedience and 'tis a fresh aggravation.   Get you home I say agen.   Get you gon home, & Elect ye Bishop of Oxford or else you must expect to feel the heavy hand of an angry King.

Then the Fellows offered their Petit͞con agen on their knees.

K. Begon, I will receive nothing from you until you have obey'd me & Elect the B. of Oxford.

‘ Uppon which they went directly to their Chapple & Dr Pudsey proposing whether they would obey ye King & elect ye B: of Ox. They all answered in their turns, that they were as ready to obey His Maj^{ty} in all things that lay in their power as any of his Subjects but electing ye B: of Oxford being directly contrary to their statutes & to the positive Oathes they had sworne thereto ; they

could

could not apprehend it to be in their power to obey him in that matter. Only Mr. Dobson answered doubtingly y^t he was ready to obey him in everything he could, & Mr. Chernock ye Papist was for obeying him in that.

' I am glad to hear the Gun has pleased you so well. The post just going, therefore I must beg your pardon if (wth my service to Mr. Knight) I abruptly subscribe myself,—Your most obliged humble servant,

Ox. 13th Septr 87. ' J. FISHER.'

The further course of political events at this critical period is illustrated by two other documents in the family archives. In June 1688 Lord Montagu writes to John Lewkenor informing him of the news of the birth of a ' hopefull sonn ' to the King. He was bidden to pass on the joyful news to all Corporations, Deputy Lieutenants, &c., that they may join at the appointed time ' as well in solemne thanksgiving to Almighty God for the inestimable Blessing as in such other Expressions of publick rejoiceing as are suitable for so great an occasion.'

Within a few months of this letter Lord Montagu has ceased to act as Lord Lieutenant, and the Duke of Somerset, in the absence of a legal Lord Lieutenant, considers it his duty to write from Petworth to Sir William Morley (who had married Lewkenor's mother) ordering the disarming of Papists. The letter proceeds :—

' The surprizing news I received by an express last night from London y^t ye King was taken on board his yatch by some Fishermen wch did not know it was him till they brought him

R

him ashoar and y^t he was known by severall who sent to ye L^ds at London to know w^t to doe for He would feign have gone aboard againe, but ye L^ds sent his coaches & guards for him to bring him to London so y^t I being sent for I shall & all ye world will judge now how ye world will goe, wch w^n I am ceirtaine off any thing I will send down intelligence into ye country.—I am y^r Humble Servant,

'SOMMERSET.'

We have allowed ourselves this long digression on the Lewkenors both because it is taken from original documents bearing on important events in English history, and also because the Lewkenors occupied an influential position in the story of the Chawton estate. They were ancestors of three successive owners of the Manor and the bulk of their property descended to them.

MARTIN

Sa. a chevron between three doves or martlets ar.

We saw in the last chapter that the male line of Knights came to an end with Sir Richard. His father's sister Dorothy had married Michael Martin of Ensham in Oxfordshire. The Martins were settled at Ensham, near Witney, in the reign of Henry VIII, as is shown by the following extract from an ancient record :—

'These were the ancient Armes or badges of Honor conferred upon Jason Martyn of or nere Witney in the County of Oxon Esqr. by Henry the Eighth of England for service by the said Martyn done in the said King's expedition to Bulloine viz.

Sable

Richard Knight

Christopher Knight

Sable a chevron between three doves argent. For the crest (creast) A Cockatrice displayed or the wreath sable argent.

'(Signed) WM. RYLEY, NORROY.'

The son of Michael Martin and Dorothy Knight, another Michael, married the Frances Lewkenor mentioned above, and it was to their son Richard that Sir Richard Knight devised his property, with remainder to Richard's brother and sister, Christopher and Elizabeth, and with the proviso that any one of them succeeding to it should take the name of Knight instead of Martin.

Sir Richard also directed his executors to lay out £500 on raising a monument to him in Chawton Church; the money for this and for the payment of his debts and legacies was to be provided by the sale of the woods. The loss of the woods, however, was averted by the generosity of Michael Martin, the heir's father, who bought them for £4600 and left them standing for his son.

It seems that during the minority of the heir the mansion was let for a time to Lord Wiltshire, son of the Marquess of Winchester (afterwards first Duke of Bolton). A MS. notebook in the possession of Lord Bolton gives the names of three of the Paulet family as having been born at Chawton in the years 1684, 1685, and 1686, one of them being Charles, afterwards third Duke of Bolton, the husband of Lavinia Fenton.

Young Richard went up to Oxford and died of smallpox, while an undergraduate at Christ Church, in 1687.

His brother Christopher had a somewhat longer tenure of the

the property, but he died unmarried in 1702 at the age of thirty-three ; and no wonder, poor man ! considering the apothecary's bill which was paid after his death by his sister— more than £40 expended on boluses, cordial potions, and fomentations, and all used in the last three months of his life.

AUTOGRAPH OF CHRISTOPHER KNIGHT

His successor, his sister Elizabeth, occupies a central position in the history of Chawton. She reigned for thirty-five years ; she survived two husbands ; and circumstances gave her the power to settle the destination of a large landed property for generations to come. We picture her to ourselves as a woman of strong character, masterful but affectionate, and with a keen sense of the duties—as well as of the dignity —of her position. She was somewhat of a *grande Dame*, and her progresses were marked by the ringing of church bells ; but her accounts, which are very carefully kept, record not only large gifts to churches and individuals, but also many unostentatious acts of charity. A few extracts from the correspondence which has been preserved will serve to illustrate both her character and her social surroundings. It was a society which did not despise gossip, and which was by no means destitute of humour. As soon as she had succeeded to the estate she wrote the following frank and somewhat imperious letter to her woodman.

'12th December, 1702.

'JOHN NAISH,—I am very sorrey to hear y^t you are ye Occasion of giving yourself and me so much trouble concerning y^r putting Cattle into ye Woods wch I have continuall Intelligence of—likewise a great many sheep mark wth y^r own name—wch is a thing I will not suffer I doe asure you therefore dont provoke one that is so Inclinable to be y^r ffriend provided I find you just to me.

'I know you will aledge y^t you have enemies y^t give me y^s Information but I hear it from so maney y^t I must beleive it therefore I would advice you to Lett it be so no more—and now John I must tell you y^t I signed y^r account when in Town because you tould me it was by my Dear Brothers orders wch is what I must always have a Regarde to, but for ye futer I expect an account in ye Distinct maner following,' &c.

John Naish was evidently unable to satisfy her, for in the next month she calls upon him to deliver his account to a successor whom she has already appointed.

In August 1718 Elizabeth writes to her 'Cousin Gardiner,' who had recently lost her husband, and whose marriage settlement was in Elizabeth's custody. She begs her cousin 'not to indulge y^r grief so much to Destroy y^r health wch is Valluable to all y^r friends, particularly myself.' She goes on to speak of a recent will, some' of the provisions of which made her think very badly of the testator. 'I always took him,' she said, 'for an Honest Gentleman but cannot help thinking, by

y^s

yᵉ Act, but that he has made his name Infamous to all Posterity: I talk like an Old-fashion person for I think Religion and Justness grows out of date.' Cousin Gardiner answers to Elizabeth's husband William. She speaks of her grief and loss but is able to turn away to subjects of a more trivial nature. Of another cousin of hers she says : ' Shee is better but looks sadley still, her Daughters and shee are parted, wich I thinke will be much for the better, for Poor Woman shee may say as my deare Mr. Gardiner used to doe His Olive Branches Had Maney Thorn's,—Lady Chathrin Sidney has Marry'd herselfe to a Capt not worth a Groat.—Lady Munson has tooke a Hous in yᵉ Pell Mall two Little Rooms of a floor and a Closet for wᶜʰ Shee gives a hundred and twenty pound a yeare— without a Coachhous or stables, but then it looks into yᵉ Parke—Mrs. Stonehouse S. John's sister has discretley marry'd her footman,' &c.

But what, we wonder, is the meaning of the following quasi-legal document ? It looks as if it were an elaborate joke invented to relieve the tedium of a wet day in the country, but Edward Mumford was the steward, and hardly likely to take part in a joke with the lady of the Manor, while the other two parties to it, though they bear the name of Martin and Lewkenor, cannot now be identified as individuals. Anyhow, the document is redolent of the period.

' West Deane, Augᵗ 20th 1722.

' I do hereby irrevocably authorize and desire my Worthy friends Mrs. Knight (Lady of West Deane) Philip Meniconi of Sunbury

Emery Walker ph. sc.

Eliz: Knight

Sunbury Esq, Mr. Edward Bowman of London and my deare
Wife Laura Martin joyntly & severally to Pull me out of
Bed, or beat me, or take such other measures as they or any
of them shall judge proper, for the rousing and recovering me
from the spleen ; and for so doing this shall be a sufficient
Warrant & authority and also a testamony of my thanks
for it.

'WM. MARTIN.'

Witness :   Ed: Lewkenor
            Ed: Mumford.

Elizabeth's first husband (to whom she appears to have
been warmly attached) was her first cousin, William Woodward,
whose mother had been Elizabeth Lewkenor.   The pair became
the sole representatives of the Lewkenors,
the last John Lewkenor having died
without issue, and left the bulk of his
property to them.   In consequence of
having succeeded to Westdean, Woodward
had to serve the Office of High Sheriff for
Sussex in 1709, having already occupied
a similar position in Surrey as the owner
of Fosters (the Woodwards' place) in 1702.   The office
must have been something of a burden, if one may judge
from a letter written by Woodward to his cousin John
Lewkenor.

WOODWARD

Barry of six az. and
ar., three bucks' heads
cabossed or.

'March y^e 30th 1703.

'SR,—I received of Hugh Madely 22 Guineas for which I return you and y^e Lady Morley my humble and hearty thanks. Nothing could have been more acceptable to a Sheriff except his Quietus est, and nothing more welcome to me except your good company. By the little value you have for ye Town I'me almost satisfy'd you are grown a very Stoick, therefore (having read y^t Diogenes preferr'd a Tubb before a Kingdom), I've presum'd to send you one with Sturgeon. May you be Philosopher enough to think it so, if not I can never repay the manifold favours I've receiv'd. Having already troubled you with a Tale of a Tubb I referr you to Mr Ford to give an account of ye Assizes I shall onely beg leave to say that if any one thing was well or honorable it must be wholly attributed to ye noble and generous present you kindly bestow'd on—Your most humble servant,

'WM. WOODWARD.

'Pray my service to all.'

Woodward died in 1721. Four years later Mrs. Elizabeth was remarried to Bulstrode Peachey, brother of Sir John Peachey of Petworth. Both her husbands took the name of Knight on their marriage, and both were members of Parliament for Midhurst. This borough was probably subject to the influence of the Lewkenors, an influence which would have passed to Elizabeth and her first husband jointly, and to herself after his death. She survived her second husband two years

PEACHEY
Az. a lion ramp. double-
queued erm.; on a canton
ar. a mullet pierced gu.

years (1735–1737), and (in spite of her release from an uncongenial partner) they must have been years of much solitude and melancholy. Not only had she outlived both her brothers and both her husbands, but there were no nephews or nieces— no near relatives, in fact, of any sort, to enliven her old age. She had to seek for a successor among those of whom she knew comparatively little, and who might be indifferent to the traditions of the place where she had spent the greater part of her life ; and in making the disposition which she felt obliged to make of her estate she must have deeply regretted having to nominate persons who did not belong to the old family of Knight. The regret would have been still greater had she known that nearly a century would elapse before Chawton again became the regular settled home of the family.

SILVER SCALLOP-SHELL BELONGING TO MRS. ELIZABETH KNIGHT

PEDIGREE IV.—MAYS

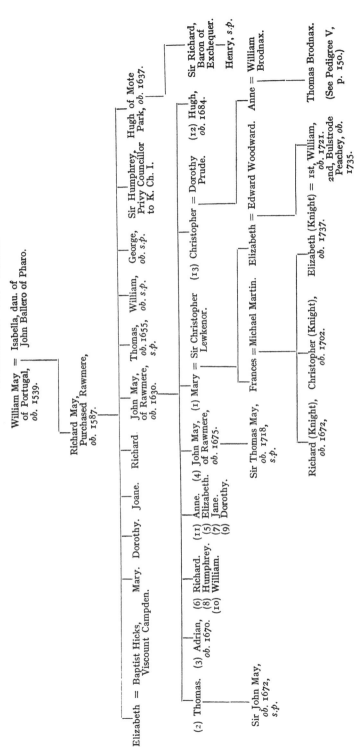

BOOK PLATE OF BAPTIST MAY, JUNR.

CHAPTER VI

THE MAYS AND THE BRODNAXES

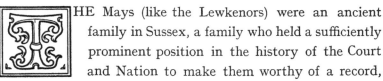

HE Mays (like the Lewkenors) were an ancient family in Sussex, a family who held a sufficiently prominent position in the history of the Court and Nation to make them worthy of a record, and who are especially interesting to us from the important place they occupy in the smaller history of Chawton.

The elder branch of the family, who became owners of Pashly in the middle of the sixteenth century, do not specially concern us, but one of them deserves more than a passing mention. This Thomas May, who is described[1] as the eldest

son

---

[1] *Dictionary of National Biography,* s.v.

son of Sir Thomas May of Mayfield, Sussex, was educated
at Sidney Sussex College, Cambridge, and evidently imbibed
there a great love for the classics.   He was for a time at the
Court of Charles I, where he became an intimate friend of the
versatile Endymion Porter.   But a cause of offence arose—
'some disgust,' Fuller tells us ('Worthies of Sussex'), 'was
given to or taken by him (as some will have it) because his
bays were not gilded richly enough and his verses rewarded
by King Charles according to his expectations'; these verses
having included no less than five plays.   May thereupon left
the Court for the Parliament, and abandoned poetry for prose.
He became the historian of the Long Parliament, but he had
the merit of not showing the bitterness of a renegade.   He tells
us in his Preface that he has endeavoured to avoid partiality,
and that if he says more of Roundheads than of Cavaliers
it is merely because he had better sources of information on
that side, and adds, 'If those that write on the other side
will use the same candour, there is no feare but that posterity
may receive a full information concerning the unhappy dis-
tractions of these kingdoms.'   Perhaps Professor Firth was
right in saying that May deserves praise 'rather for the moderation of his language than for the independence of his views';
but at all events he has the distinction of having pleased
Lord Chatham, who advised his nephew to read May's History
as 'much honester and more instructive than Clarendon's.'   A
less pleasant impression is, we are told, produced by the
contrast between his 'History of the Parliament,' written
when he was endeavouring to please the Parliamentary Party,
and

and his ' Breviary of the History of the Parliament,' in which he made the cause of the Army and the Independents his own.

Thomas May died suddenly in 1652, and was buried in Westminster Abbey near a historian who was much more to Fuller's liking, viz. Camden. ' If he were,' says Fuller, ' a biassed and partiall writer he lieth near a good and true historian.' Had Fuller written after the Restoration he would have been obliged to add that the bones of May, with those of the others of the defeated party, were ejected from the Abbey, and cast into a pit in St. Margaret's Churchyard.

Meanwhile a younger branch of the May family had acquired property at Rawmere near Chichester. The ancestor of these, William, settled in Portugal, where he married Isabella, daughter of John Ballero or Balliro of Pharo. William May himself died in Portugal (1539), but his sons were naturalised in England, and Richard, the eldest of them, purchased Rawmere about 1580. This Richard had a large family, of whom the most distinguished, Sir Humphrey May, was a Privy Councillor, and also, apparently, Chancellor of the Duchy of Lancaster and Vice-Chamberlain to Charles I. He was a Courtier, but on the side of moderation and conciliation, and while in Parliament he ' displayed conspicuous talent as a debater and tactician.' In addition to holding the offices which we have mentioned, he had the reversion of the Mastership of

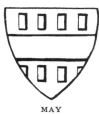

MAY
Gu. a fess between eight billets or.

of the Rolls, but did not live to enjoy it. Altogether he was evidently a very notable person, but he was only a cadet of the family and must have been quite a little boy in 1585, when his sister Elizabeth was married to that remarkable product of the Elizabethan age, Baptist Hicks, who began life as a silk-mercer and money-lender and ended it as Viscount Campden. A long account of him will be found in Mrs. Hicks Beach's interesting book ' A Cotswold Family.' It was a time when social ambitions had a fair chance of being gratified, for the old Peerage of England, reduced to small dimensions by the Wars of the Roses, was being freely replenished out of the numerous families who rose to affluence under the Tudors. Certainly no hard-and-fast line was drawn between the possession of land and the pursuit of trade in that restless and enterprising age. Baptist Hicks and Elizabeth May were both born of citizen parents (for Richard May was Master of the Merchant Taylors' Company) ; and Baptist feels no shame in continuing to supply hangings for James I's Coronation, and lending money to Scottish nobles (whom he describes as ' fayre speakers and slow performers ' in the way of paying their debts) : while his brother Michael is acting as private secretary to Burghley and Robert Cecil. The path is open to Baptist from his shop to a knighthood, a baronetcy, a seat in several Parliaments, a peerage and a palace in Gloucestershire. The site of his house behind Kensington parish church he is said to have acquired by the easy process of winning it at cards. If so, it was a curious beginning to a name which has lasted so long as that of Campden Hill. Baptist left no son, but his

peerage

Hugh May

From a miniature by Samuel Cooper

peerage descended to the husband of one of his daughters. Meanwhile the ownership of Rawmere passed, in the first instance, to the eldest brother of Elizabeth and Humphrey May, viz. Richard ; but it was afterwards, by a family arrangement, transferred to John.   John, again, had many children— one often wonders what becomes of all these successive large families, which seem amply sufficient to guarantee the preservation of the race—and some of them must detain us for a short time.   The property at Rawmere passed from John to his eldest son Thomas, but eventually on the failure of his issue it went to Thomas's brother John, and thereafter to John's son, Sir Thomas May, who died without issue in 1718.   But much the most distinguished son of the first-mentioned John was Hugh, the celebrated architect, and the friend of John Evelyn. An excellent miniature of him, painted by Samuel Cooper in 1653, depicts him as a young man with a delicate and thoughtful countenance.   He wears a slight moustache and is dressed in the costume which we are in the habit of associating with the reign of Charles II.   On his shoulder is a blue cloak, cast loosely over a dark coat.

Hugh May designed on a large scale, and was concerned in many of the important buildings of his time ; and a further point of interest is that in some of his works he was associated with Grinling Gibbons.   May was one of a distinguished party who went over the old Cathedral of St. Paul's, less than a week before the fire of London,[1] to ' survey the generall decays of that
ancient

---

[1] *Evelyn's Diary*, 27 August 1666 ; 1 March 1671 ; 25 August 1672 ; 18 April 1680.

ancient & venerable Church & to set downe in writing the
particulars of what was fit to be don, with the charge thereof,
giving our opinions from article to article '; but we are not
informed what part he took in the wordy contest which ensued,
between Dr. Wren and Mr. Evelyn on one side, and
Mr. Chichley and Mr. Prat on the other, during which Dr. Wren
and Mr. Evelyn (we may presume the initiative came from
the former) unfolded the idea of ' a noble cupola, a form
of Church-building not as yet known in England, but of
wonderful grace.'

The following extracts from ' Evelyn's Diary ' show that
he took great interest in his friend's work, but, at the same
time, that with him friendship did not preclude free criticism.

Speaking of Mr. Gibbons, he says (1st March 1671) : ' His
Majesties surveyor Mr. Wren faithfully promis'd me to employ
him.   I have also bespoke his Majesty for his worke at Windsor,
which my friend Mr. May the architect there is going to alter
& repair universally.'

' 1672. *Aug. 25.*—I dined at Lord John Berkley newly
ariv'd out of Ireland where he had ben Deputy ; it was in
his new house or rather Palace, for I am assur'd it stood him
in neere £30,000.   It is very well built and has many noble
roomes but they are not very convenient consisting but of one
Corps de Logis, they are all roomes of state without clossets.
The staircase is of cedar, the furniture is princely : the kitchen
& stables are ill-plac'd, and the corridor worse, having no
report to the wings they joyne to.   For the rest, the forecourt
is noble, so are the stables, and above all, the gardens.   The
holly hedge on the terrace I advised the planting of.   The

Porticos

Porticos are in imitation of an house described by Palladio, but it happens to be the worst in his booke, tho' my good friend Mr. Hugh May, his Lordship's Architect, effected it.'

Under date 18th April 1680 he describes the seat of the Earl of Essex, Cashioberie. ' The House,' he says, ' is a plaine fabric, built by my friend Mr. Hugh May. There are diver's faire and good roomes and excellant carving by Gibbons especialy the chimney piece of the Library. . . .'

' I did not approve of the middle dores being round but when the Hall is finish'd as design'd it being an oval with a cupola together with the other wing it will be a very noble palace.'

Hugh May expected to succeed Sir John Denham as Surveyor of Works ; but in 1667 the post was given to Wren, and May was promised an annuity of £300 as a solatium. In 1683 he was building a house at Chiswick for Sir Stephen Fox ; and this must have been almost his last work, for he died in 1684. He had several brothers and sisters in addition to those we have already mentioned. One of them, Mary,[1] married, as her second husband, Sir Christopher Lewkenor, the defender of Chichester whose acquaintance we have already made in the last chapter. The youngest brother, Christopher May, married Dorothy Prude, and their daughter Anne married William Brodnax of Godmersham Park, near Canterbury.

The reader must be so good as to take notice of these Lewkenor and Brodnax marriages, as the subsequent disposition of the Chawton property depends on them.

There

[1] For an account of the circumstances connected with this marriage see pp. 115 and 116.

T

There were other prominent members of the May family in the seventeenth century. Sir Humphrey's kinsmen benefited by his high position at Court : at any rate, Sir Algernon was Keeper of the Records, and Baptist (whose picture is at Chawton) was Keeper of the Privy Purse to Charles II, an office which was, unfortunately, incompatible with the preservation of dignity and self-respect. As for this ' Bab May,' we fear it must be admitted that Pepys, who was not likely to be particularly squeamish, speaks of his ' wicked crew ' : though he tells us elsewhere that he was one of the best tennis-players in England. Meanwhile Sir Humphrey's brother, an elder Hugh May, of Mote Park in Berkshire, had a son who became Sir Richard May, Baron of the Exchequer, and Recorder of Chichester. Of his family we need only add that his son Henry, also Recorder of Chichester, dying without issue, left his property to go with the rest of the May estate.

Altogether, the Mays seemed to have the ball at their feet during the seventeenth century. The favour of more than one sovereign, successful marriages resulting in numerous issue, and the secure possession of landed property—all seemed likely to assure the prosperity and continuance of the race. They might have been expected to take an important place in the struggles of the great families which characterise the politics of the eighteenth century. So far, however, is this from being the case that, in the eighteenth century, the Mays entirely disappear ; and we must now follow the fortunes of the Brodnaxes, whose lot it was to represent the branch of the Mays living at Rawmere.

The

The family of Brodnax[1] settled in Romney Marsh in the first half of the fifteenth century. Samuel Pegge boldly conjectures that the name was derived from Bradnynch in Devonshire. However that may be, in 1440 Robert Brodnax was the husband of Alicia Scappe and succeeded to her father's property at Burmarsh. Their son Robert, whose will bears date November 1487, was followed by his son John and his grandson William in direct succession. William's son Thomas, born 1526, was the first of the family to possess Godmersham. Mr. John Philipot, the Herald, in his 'Villare Cantianum,' gives this account of him : ' Edward Lord Clinton not long after 4th Edw. VI

BRODNAX
Or two chevrons gu.;
on a chief of the second
three cinquefoils ar.

conveyed Saltwood to Mr. Thomas Brodnax, whose family was of good repute and antiently possessed of a spreading Revenue about Burmarsh and St Maries in Romney Marsh ; and he being transplanted to Godmersham passed this Manor away to Knatchbull, who in the 18th year of Q. Eliz. alienated it to Crispe.'

This ' transplantation ' of Thomas Brodnax to Godmersham was brought about by the purchase of that place from Richard Astyn of West Peckham in the County of Kent. One is tempted to connect Richard Astyn (whose name in the spelling of those days was interchangeable with Austin and Austen) with

---

[1] Our information respecting the Brodnax family is principally derived from a manuscript history and genealogy compiled in the eighteenth century by Samuel Pegge, LL.D., the author of several works of antiquarian research.

with the tenants of St. Augustine's Abbey in the past, and with the Austens of the future, who were eventually to succeed the Brodnaxes in the possession of Godmersham, but we fear there is no sufficient evidence to support either conjecture. Thomas, the purchaser, died in 1602 and was succeeded by another Thomas, his eldest son by his second wife Julian Brockman, to the exclusion of his two elder sons by the first marriage. This gentleman, says Pegge, was pleased to become a violent Republican at the time of the Grand Rebellion and was a Captain in the Parliamentary service. A letter is extant, addressed to him from Eastwell by his neighbour, Nathaniel Finch, in which the writer excuses himself from furnishing a required quota of men for the Parliamentary army, on the ground that he had really ceased to be owner of the estate. Another document contains an undertaking on the part of Lord Finch (to whom the estate had perhaps been conveyed) that he would be faithful to ' Comon-wealth of England as it is now established, without a King or House of Lords.'

During these troublous times Brodnax transferred his place of residence to Canterbury, where he lived within the precincts of the Church, in one of the prebendal houses which he had bought. Nor was this the only Church property of which he became possessed. He also bought woodland at Godmersham described as ' late parcel of the Possessions of the late Dean and Chapter of the late Cathedral Church of Christ Church, Canterbury,' and either he or his son purchased the Manor of that place. We may be sure, however, that they

were

were not allowed to retain these possessions after the Restoration. Thomas Brodnax died at his house at Canterbury in the year 1658, aged ninety.

His son Thomas, who succeeded him, was a partner with him in those acts against the Crown ; but upon the Restoration of King Charles II he availed himself of the general pardon promised by the Declaration of Breda. His own pardon under the great seal was dated 13th May, 13th of Charles II, and the family no doubt soon resumed the habits and ideas more usually associated with country squires. Of Thomas himself we hear no more than that he died in 1667, aged sixty-eight ; but his son William was knighted about the year 1664, and married Mary Digges, of Chilham Castle, granddaughter of Sir Dudley Digges, who was a well-known Master of the Rolls, and who built the present house at Chilham.

There must have been at this time more offshoots of the house of Brodnax, at and about Godmersham, than we can now identify. In a letter written 17th August 1904, from Manchester, Virginia, Dr. John W. Brodnax mentions a Bible brought from England by his ancestor, William Brodnax, which contains the following entry : ' Wm. Brodnax, youngest son of Robert Brodnax, Goldsmith, Holborn, London, was Born at Godmersham in Kent, Feb. 28, 1675.' ' This was my dear Father's bible, Robert Brodnax ; I desire it may be given to my eldest son after my decease to keep in memory of my Grandfather and me.'

Perhaps this Robert Brodnax was a descendant of one of the two elder sons of Thomas the purchaser, who (as we have seen)

seen) did not succeed to Godmersham. If so, the future was
not devoid of its compensations, for his family became possessed
of a good estate in Virginia ; and it is pleasant to be able to
add that ' the descendants of the Brodnaxes in America have
without exception been Gentlemen of high character and
worth.' Peaceful pursuits had now been resumed at Godmersham. A copy of Evelyn's ' Kalendarium Hortense ' now at
Chawton, carefully annotated by ' Wm. Brodnax,' bears witness
to the care and love of the squire for scientific gardening.

We are now approaching the place where the family of
Brodnax fit in with our previous history ; for the son of Sir
William Brodnax and Mary Digges was the Colonel William
Brodnax who (as we have seen) married Anne May. The
death of her cousin, Sir Thomas May,[1] in 1718 left her one of
the natural representatives of her family, and it soon appeared
that by his will Sir Thomas May had devised the estate of
Rawmere (after the death of his widow) to Anne's son,
Thomas Brodnax.

Lady May died in 1726, and in the next year Thomas
Brodnax (who had lost both of his parents and was already
in the possession of Godmersham) assumed the name of May.
He was now a rich man and could afford in 1732 to commence the
great work of building the present mansion at Godmersham Park.

But he had not yet received all his promotions, nor finished
his changes of name. His mother's aunt, Mary May, wife of Sir
Christopher Lewkenor, the defender of Chichester, was grandmother of Mrs. Elizabeth Knight, now reigning at Chawton.
                                                        This

----

[1] See page 135.

From a painting by D'Agh

Emery Walker Ph. x.

Tho: Knight

This lady was therefore second cousin to Thomas Brodnax, and when she was left, after the death of her second husband, without any natural heir, she fixed upon him as her successor. She was of a disposition to value both his sterling qualities and also his more adventitious advantages of wealth and position. He would represent the family creditably, and she could provide in her will for the continuance of the family name. But she perhaps overlooked the fact that he already possessed a home to which he was warmly attached, and the probability that even the expression of her strong desire for regular residence during half the year at Chawton would be insufficient to overcome his prepossession for Godmersham. This proved to be the case, and occasional business visits (especially when the line taken by the Squire was so unpopular as the attempted sale of the Church bells) [1] were hardly likely to endear him to the tenants. His absence, however, gave the opportunity for frequent letters to pass between him and his stewards, some of which have been preserved.

The Rawmere steward writes to him (July 1740) of the 'Hanover' rats which had lately made their appearance. One of the tenants tells him, that last year they killed ' above six hundred notwithstanding which they still swarm again there still ; everybody hereabouts complains of harm done by them. They lye abroade and berry like Rabits, eate the Corn, mostly wheat, in the Barns, and Beans in the Gardens, and they are prodigious mischievious Creatures.'

On 29th March 1745, Mr. Thomas Knight writes to his
steward

---

[1] See Chapter III.

steward Randall at Chawton, telling him to accommodate a friend named Bathurst, who landed at Southampton under circumstances which obliged him to be in private. ' If he comes to Chawton he may lie in my Chamber, and I would have him dine in the parlour or in the Breakfast-Room, as he chooses, and the maid to wait on him, and let there be something dress'd for him everyday, as he likes, which your wife may always ask him, and get it accordingly, and let her buy a little good green tea and sugar for his breakfasts : in short let him be taken care of, and have what he wants, and I'll pay for everything he has. You must tell him you have no wine, but let him have strong beer as he likes, and you may buy a Bottle or two of Brandy and a few Lemons, and he'll make himself a little punch sometimes if he likes it.' Directions for concealment of his name and arrangements as to letters follow.

On 31st December 1745, Mr. Knight writes Randall an ordinary letter about poachers ; but the letter is dated ' St. James's Square in Westminster,' and the first sentence is, ' I received yours of 24th at Godmersham, but our neighbourhood there being much alarm'd about the French intending to land there, I have been in some hurry to remove my family to London.' ' There ' is a little vague, for Godmersham is a good way from any sea-coast ; but if the French were going to seize Dover, or to sail up the Thames, they would in either case have come unpleasantly near.

In March 1746 he writes to Randall giving detailed instructions as to the furniture of Rawmere which was to be moved to Chawton : and it is a curious note of the times, and perhaps

of

From a painting by D'Aigh   Emery Walker Ph.sc.

Jane Knight

of the economical disposition of the writer, that much is said as to the windows to be stopped up in the dismantled house of Rawmere in consequence of the window tax. They were to be stopped up 'with lath and plaister at the Inside and the Glass left at the Outside.'

On 13th June 1748 he condoles with Randall on the death of his son by drowning off the coast of China. ' By going out of the Ship in the Boat, as they lay in the River Canton, his foot slip't and he fell into the Water, and tho' there was help enough at hand, he never rose again for them to save him ; and it is a remarkable Quality of the Water, that a person falling does not rise ; and Mr. Robinson says, he has lost another man there who went into the River to wash, and these two are all he has lost in the voyage. I know this must be grief to you and Mrs. Randall, but you must inform her of it in the gentlest manner you can ; and it must be a comfort to you that you did your part in bringing him up, and have provided for him in the best manner you could, and that he received his Fate by the hand of Providence, to which we must all submit.'

The gentleman of whom we have been speaking, who bore successively the names of Brodnax, May, and Knight, was educated at Balliol College, Oxford. He then studied law, and, after acting as High Sheriff of Kent in 1729, he became in 1734 M.P. for Canterbury. Meanwhile, in July 1729, he had married Jane, daughter and co-heiress of William Monke of

KNIGHT
Vert a bend lozengy or, in base a cinquefoil ar.

of Buckingham House, Shoreham, Sussex, a lady whose connexion with the subsequent owners of Godmersham and Chawton will be described in the next chapter. Mr. Knight died in 1781 ; ' a gentleman,' says Hasted, ' whose eminent worth ought not here to pass unnoticed; whose high character for upright conduct and integrity stamped a universal confidence and authority on all he said and did, which rendered his life as honourable as it was good, and caused his death to be lamented by everyone as a public loss.' [1]

In the course of his life he parted with the two properties Rawmere and Westdean, both near Chichester, the old homes of the Mays and Lewkenors respectively. The former he sold outright ; the latter was exchanged for the properties of Neatham and Colmer near Chawton.

Among the articles of furniture and house-decoration transferred from Westdean to Chawton is a large piece of tapestry.[2] It is probably French, and it was executed in 1564 for the family of Lewkenor. The tapestry contains the Lewkenor Arms and in addition, the following coats of families connected with them—Tregoz, Camoys, Culpeper, Audley, Touchet, Dalingrig, Grimsted, D'Oyley, Delawarr and Cantilupe, Moyne, Bruse, Gournay, and Pelham. The family evidently set great store by this piece of work, for Sir John Lewkenor in a document dated 1662 gives the following injunction to his heirs : ' Remenber to keep safe ye Carpet of Armes, now aged about 100 yeares, w^ch, in y^e failure of the elder house totalie

consuming

---

[1] Hasted's *History of Kent*, 1790, vol. 3, p. 159 (b).

[2] The tapestry measures sixteen feet three inches in length by seven feet two inches in width.

CARPET OF ARMS

consuming itselfe by daughters & heires & passing into other
names, was sent hither by Constance Glemham of Trotton,
who was one of those heires, for record to the younger house
and whole name.'

Mr. and Mrs. Knight had a considerable family, but several
died in infancy. Of those that grew up three daughters never
married, and the only son, Thomas, succeeded his father in
his estates.

Thomas Knight the second seems to have been cast in a
slightly different mould from his father ; with equal self-
respect and sense of responsibility for his public actions, he
had more sweetness and less self-assertion. He was educated
at Eton, and his name figures in the recently reprinted Eton
school lists. Thence he was entered at Magdalen College,
Oxford ; and he seems to have taken his academical life
seriously, for it is mentioned that in 1755 he made a speech in
the Sheldonian Theatre. His enduring love for his University
was shown by his bequests of four cabinets of English coins,
and also of a cornelian set in silver, taken from the body of
Hampden after his death on Chalgrove field, on which are
inscribed the words :

> Against my King I do not fight,
> But for my King and Kingdom's right.

In 1759 he received the degree of M.A., and afterwards made
the tour of Europe so indispensable for the finished gentleman
of that age. On his return he became M.P. for New Romney,
and as such one of the Barons of the Cinque Ports. A little
silver gilt bell preserved at Chawton (which may be seen on

p. 149)

p. 149) is a reminiscence of the Coronation of George III. These bells were part of the ornament of the canopy held over the King's head by the Barons of the Cinque Ports. Mr. Knight was subsequently M.P. for Kent, but in 1780 he withdrew from public business, a year before his father's death, and a year after his own marriage to Catherine, daughter of the Rev. Wadham Knatchbull, Rector of Chilham and Prebendary and Chancellor of Durham. Mr. Knight spent the rest of his life in the quiet performance of his duties as a country gentleman.

' It gives my Wife and myself great pleasure,' writes a friend of his in 1789, ' when we reflect on the Happiness, peace in Mind, and Health, we hope and believe Mrs. Knight and you enjoy in your pleasant Mansion, and Situation ; tho' I often wish your Inclination had prompted you to have continued longer in a more active Life ; there are now so few, who act on benevolent principles, that a worthy and good man's retirement from the Active part of life, must be a loss to his Country. In every other respect, domestic Happyness, a good Situation, and a good library, are the most desirable things in this world.' And the following account was published at the time of his death : ' His Carriage & address were those of a man of fashion, & his temper serene accompanied by a friendly disposition equally candid & sincere. His understanding was sound & well cultivated & his conversation abounded with a facetious pleasantry ; which rendered his company universally acceptable.' [1]

He and his wife must have been indeed delightful persons

to

[1] *Gentleman's Magazine*, November 1794.

Emory Walker Ph. sc.

Geo Romney   Thoˢ Knight

to meet, if they at all resembled (as no doubt they did) the two beautiful portraits by Romney, now at Chawton, one of which forms the frontispiece of this book, while the other is to be found opposite to this page.   Mr. Knight died at Chawton, 23rd October 1794.   He left no issue and his disposition of the estates of Godmersham and Chawton will form a principal subject of the next chapter.   We will only add here that it is certain, from her subsequent course of action, that Mrs. Knight was a willing co-operator with her husband in the measures which he took to secure an eventual successor to the estate.

BELL USED AT CORONATION OF GEORGE III

PEDIGREE V.—AUSTENS

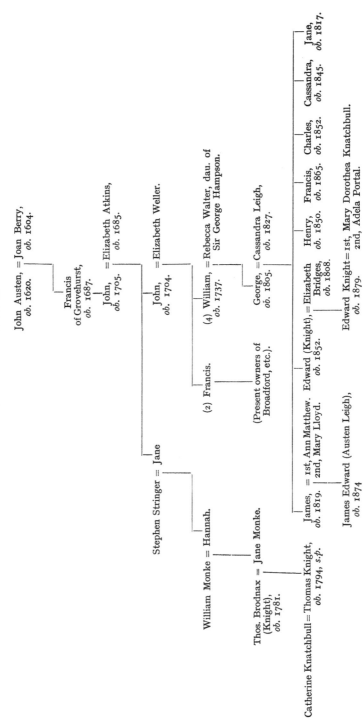

John Austen, = Joan Berry,
ob. 1620.   ob. 1604.

Francis
of Grovehurst,
ob. 1687.

John, = Elizabeth Atkins,
ob. 1705.   ob. 1685.

John, = Elizabeth Weller.
ob. 1704.

Stephen Stringer = Jane

(2) Francis.

(4) William, = Rebecca Walter, dau. of
ob. 1737.   Sir George Hampson.

William Monke = Hannah.

(Present owners of
Broadford, etc.).

George, = Cassandra Leigh,
ob. 1805.   ob. 1827.

Thos. Brodnax = Jane Monke.
(Knight),
ob. 1781.

James, = 1st, Ann Matthew.   Edward (Knight), = Elizabeth   Henry,   Francis,   Charles,   Cassandra,   Jane,
ob. 1819.   2nd, Mary Lloyd.   ob. 1852.   Bridges,   ob. 1850.   ob. 1865.   ob. 1852.   ob. 1845.   ob. 1817.
                                                          ob. 1808.

Catherine Knatchbull = Thomas Knight,
ob. 1794, s.p.

James Edward (Austen Leigh),   Edward Knight = 1st, Mary Dorothea Knatchbull.
ob. 1874   ob. 1879.   2nd, Adela Portal.

JANE AUSTEN'S MUSIC BOOK (DESIGN BY CIPRIANI)
AND AUTOGRAPH

CHAPTER VII

THE AUSTENS

THE family of Austen had been long settled in Kent; and the particular branch of it with which we are concerned emerges into notice early in the seventeenth century at Horsmonden in that county. There are brasses in the church of that parish to John Austen, who died in 1620, and to Joan his wife. Joan had died in 1604, after giving birth to twins who came at the end of a long family. She met her death, says the inscription, ' often utteringe these speeches, Let neither husband nor children, nor lands nor goods, separate me me from my God.' As to 'lands' we can say nothing more definite than that in the course of the seventeenth century the Austens became possessed of the two small manor houses of Broadford and Grovehurst in Horsmonden parish, both of which their descendants still own. Broadford is a picturesque

AUSTEN

Or a chevron gu. be-
tween three lions' jambs
erect erased sa.

Elizabethan residence of very moderate size, standing just above the valley. A large room on the first floor is completely panelled with oak (now whitewashed), and contains over the fireplace and elsewhere the alternate rose and carnation which are supposed to mark the Tudor age. Over the fireplace in the entrance-hall are the Austen arms, with the date 1587. When they were placed there is not known, but the date given must be anterior to the Austens' possession of Broadford. Grovehurst is about three-quarters of a mile from Broadford, and at the top of the hill. The north front of the house exhibits a charming assemblage of gables, with rough-cast below. The Austens, no doubt, made their money as clothiers, and the rollers used in the exercise of that trade may still be seen attached to the ceiling of one of the upper rooms at Broadford. The John Austens (they were nearly always christened ' John ') of that century evidently desired to take their place as squires of the county, and with the one who died, after a long reign, in 1705 this must have been a dominating motive of action. He contented himself, however, with occupying the smaller of his two houses, viz. Grovehurst ; while his son, another John,

on

on his marriage with Elizabeth Weller in 1693, was installed at Broadford.   The elder John seems to have been something of a Tartar, or at all events to have liked ruling his family as well as upholding his position ; John the younger must have been easy-going and careless, and possibly pleasure-loving. He died of consumption in 1704, and his poor wife was left in a position the difficulties of which she afterwards unfolded to her children in a memorandum still extant.   She had one daughter and six sons to maintain, and it transpired that her husband had left behind him considerable debts, of some of which she had been ignorant.   She cast around for the means of paying them, and naturally appealed in the first instance to her ' father Austen.'   He began by refusing her petition so positively that it seemed as if no expedient would be left her but a sale of her furniture.   Later on, however, he said he would give her £200 ; not enough to pay the debts, but leaving (after taking credit for certain assets) only a small sum to make up.   John the elder had just arranged to do this, when he fell ill and died.   It might have been thought that Elizabeth's position would be improved by this event ; but it appeared that the old man had tied up the estate tightly in favour of her eldest little boy ; while the executors held that they had no right to pay her the promised £200, as to which no legally binding arrangement had been concluded before the father's death.   She did, however, eventually manage to pay off the debts by the sale of a leasehold house (which seems to have been in her own power), and a few valuables, and she lived on four more years at Broadford with the children—Betty, Jack, Frank,

x

Frank, Tom, Will, Robin, and Stephen. Then the question of education began to be urgent ; there was none to be got at Horsmonden. So she decided to move to Sevenoaks (' Sennocks,' she called it) and to take a roomy house within reach of its grammar school. There she was to board the schoolmaster and some of his pupils. Her accounts go down to the time when her boys were beginning to go out into the world ; but she died in 1720, too soon to see the success which, on the whole, attended them. Jack, the Squire, had been taken off her hands when she moved to Sevenoaks. Frank was a solicitor at Tonbridge and Sevenoaks who eventually amassed a considerable fortune. While his two next brothers, Tom and Will (both of whom had adopted the medical profession) were marrying young, and on small incomes, he remained single, and acted as a good uncle to his nephews. In later life he married twice ; one of his grandsons by his first marriage was Colonel Thomas Austen, M.P. for Kent, whose second wife was a sister of Cardinal Manning ; a grandson of the second family, Rev. John Thomas Austen, was Senior Wrangler in 1817. Soon after the beginning of the nineteenth century the line of John Austen of Broadford came to an end, and the Horsmonden estate came into the possession of Frank's descendants, who still hold it. Of Frank's brothers, Tom, the doctor, married, and has left descendants in the female line, and Stephen became a well-known bookseller and publisher in London. Concerning Robin, history is silent; he probably died young.

William (the fourth brother), whose fortunes particularly
concern

concern us, was a surgeon. His profession seems to have given him an introduction into medical circles, for his wife was daughter of one M.D. and widow of another. Born in 1701, William must have married when he was twenty-seven or twenty-eight, and he seems to have chosen discreetly. Rebecca Walter was the daughter of Sir George Hampson, a doctor who had succeeded to a baronetcy, which his descendants still hold. By her first husband, Dr. Walter, she had a son, who remained on intimate terms with his half-brother and half-brother's family. Judging from the character of her son, George Austen, we may guess that Rebecca was a woman of force and intellect, but unfortunately she died in giving birth to her fourth child and third daughter in 1732–3. The eldest daughter died in infancy, the youngest unmarried. The father only lived till 1737. How the children, George, Philadelphia and Leonora, were brought up we do not exactly know ; but, at any rate, George was befriended by his uncle Frank and sent to Tonbridge School, whence he got a scholarship at St. John's College, Oxford. He became a Fellow of his College, and from his striking appearance was well known in the University as the ' Handsome Proctor.' It is a curious coincidence that by his marriage his descendants became entitled to hold—and more than one of them did hold—Fellowships at St. John's College, as Founder's kin.

His sister Philadelphia went out to India in the adventurous manner often adopted by portionless girls in the early days of the English occupation, and married a friend of Warren Hastings.

We must now return to Elizabeth Weller and her brothers-in-law.

in-law.   One of them, the husband of a Jane Austen, was Stephen Stringer of Triggs in the parish of Goudhurst.   The Wellers and the Stringers, like the Austens, seem to have been families who were stepping from trade into the ownership of land ; Stephen Stringer was High Sheriff of Kent in 1708.   Of the five daughters of Stephen and Jane Stringer, one, Mary, married her cousin John Austen, another, Hannah, married

MONKE

Gu. a chevr. between three lions' heads erased ar.

William Monke.   The Monkes were people of property near Shoreham, distantly related to George, Duke of Albemarle, and descended from the ancient family of Le Moine, of Powdridge in Devonshire.   It was therefore quite in the natural order of things that their daughter, Jane, should become the wife of the owner of Godmersham, Thomas Brodnax, afterwards Knight, whose acquaintance we have made in the last chapter.   Mr. Knight was thus second cousin by marriage to George Austen, and he acknowledged his cousinship by presenting him to the rectory of Steventon in Hants, which he had inherited, as part of the Lewkenor property, from Mrs. Elizabeth Knight.   His son was destined to be a still greater benefactor to one of his Steventon cousins.

George Austen, to whom we have now returned, was evidently a fine specimen of the parson of the eighteenth century, a class of whom hard things have often been said. Striking and refined in appearance, cultured in his tastes, beneficent, and attentive to his clerical duties, he must have

attracted

REV. GEORGE AUSTEN

MRS. GEORGE AUSTEN

attracted regard and affection wherever he was known.   Like many of his family he married with discretion.   Cassandra Leigh, daughter of the Rector of Harpsden near Henley, and granddaughter of Theophilus Leigh of Adlestrop, was vigorous, lively, and shrewd.   She had a large family and lived to an advanced age.   Her husband not only educated his own sons at home, but also took pupils ; and with these to care for, and not infrequent guests, Cassandra's time must have been fully occupied.   Hers, as we have seen,[1] was the deciding voice which sent their son Edward to pay that visit to the last Mr. and Mrs. Thomas Knight (the Mr. Thomas Knight whose father had settled the Austens at Steventon) which had such important results to the boy.   But his adoption by his patrons must have been a gradual affair.   They can only have been married a very short time when he first attracted their notice, and the idea of adopting a distant cousin as their heir would not arise till some time afterwards.

Many years later Edward Austen's niece, Caroline Austen, wrote down her reminiscences of what her uncle Henry had told her in 1848 concerning his brother Edward's early life. Henry Austen could not remember the exact date of the invitation to his brother to go to Godmersham.   Indeed, he evidently ante-dated it considerably in his own mind.   But, his niece adds, ' he was very clear as to the purport of the discourse which he heard between his Father & Mother on the morning when they received a letter from Godmersham, begging that little Edward might spend his Holidays there.

(I

_____
[1] Chap. I, p. 9.

(I suppose " Holidays " referred to those which my Grandfather's pupils had, and that his own boys were let off from
much work at the same time.)

'My grandfather was *not* disposed to consent to Mr.
Knight's request.   With the single eye of a Teacher, he looked
only at one point, which was, that, if Edward went away to
Godmersham for so many weeks he would get very much
behind in the Latin Grammar.   My grandmother seems to
have used no arguments, and to have suggested no expectations ;   she merely said, " I think, my dear, you had better
oblige your cousins, and let the child go " ;   and so he went,
and at the end of the Holidays he came back, as much Edward
Austen as before.   But after this, the Summer Holidays, at
least, were spent Aith the Knights, he being still left to his
Father's tuition.   Uncle Henry could not say when it was
announced in the family that *one* son was adopted elsewhere—
it was, in time, understood so to be ;   and he supposed that
his Parents and the Knights came to an early understanding
on the subject.   Edward Austen was more and more at Godmersham and less at Steventon, but I do not know *when* he
was entirely transferred from his Father's house to some other
place of education, and to Godmersham as a home, or whether
he ever *did* go to any sort of school, before he was finished off
in Germany.'   This ' finishing-off in Germany ' seems to have
taken the place of a university education ;   and it certainly
included a year spent at Dresden, where he was kindly received
at the Saxon Court.   Indeed, many years afterwards, when his
two eldest sons had spent some time in that city, and had,

                                                                 like

Elizabeth Austen

From a miniature by Richard Cosway

like their father, received marks of attention from the Royal family, there was a pleasant exchange of letters and presents between Prince Maximilian of Saxony and ' Edward Knight, *ci-devant* Austen.' The educational tour was afterwards extended to Rome. After his return he was no doubt more completely under the protection of his kind friends at God-mersham, and accepted as their eventual heir ; and it was under their auspices that he married in 1791 Elizabeth, daughter of Sir Brook Bridges, and was settled in a house called Rowling, belonging to the Bridges family and situated near Goodnestone. The lovely features of Mrs. Edward wusten have been pre-served to the family in a beautiful miniature by Cosway, reproduced on the opposite page ; while facing page 160 appears a miniature of her husband, taken in his old age.

The death of Mr. Thomas Knight in 1794 put Edward Austen at once in a more prominent position and opened the prospect of a further advancement. The whole of the estates, both in Kent and Hants, subject to the life interest of Mrs. Knight, were devised to him. In 1799 Mrs. Knight, in a spirit of rare generosity, resigned everything to him, reserving only to herself an annuity of £2000, and retired to a house in Canter-bury. She continued to bestow on him the interest and affection of a mother. She

KNIGHT
Vert a bend lozengy
or, in base a cinquefoil
ar., a canton gu.

survived his own wife, who died at the birth of her eleventh child in 1808. Mrs. Knight lived on till 1812, and it was not till after her death that Edward Austen took

took the name of Knight. In 1801 he had served as High Sheriff of Kent, and he continued for nearly half a century to take an active part in local county business, though he shrank from entering on a political career, and consistently declined any suggestion that he should offer himself as a candidate for Parliament ; nor did he encourage any political ambitions that his sons may have entertained.

The other members of George Austen's family must now occupy our attention. His eldest son James, Rector of Steventon after his father, was of a more literary and less practical cast than Edward. Their mother thus describes them in a letter written to her sister-in-law, Mrs. Leigh Perrot of Scarlets, Berks., in 1820, after the death of James. Edward, she says, ' has a most active mind, a clear head, and a sound judgement ; he is a man of business. That my dear James was not. Classical knowledge, literary taste, and the power of elegant composition he possessed in the highest degree ; to these Mr. Knight makes no pretensions. *Both* equally good, amiable and sweet-tempered.' We may add that James's only son, James Edward (who became James Edward Austen Leigh on succeeding to the property of his great-uncle, Mr. Leigh Perrot) inherited his father's literary tastes, and had a long and honourable career in the service of the church, besides being the biographer of his aunt Jane. Henry, successively soldier, banker, and clergyman, was apparently the most brilliant, though the least successful of the brothers. Frank and Charles were sailors—Frank self-contained, self-respecting, dignified, and devout; Charles expansive, affectionate,

From a miniature by Sir William Ross   Emery Walker Ph. sc.

affectionate, and eminently loveable; 'our own particular little brother,' as his sister Jane calls him. They both rose to be Admirals—the former to be Admiral of the Fleet ; though he lost his best chance of fame from the accident of his ship having put in for water at Gibraltar at the actual time when Trafalgar was being fought.[1] Cassandra, the elder sister, was both clever and sensible, and became a real power in the family. She lived to be an old lady, and, living at Chawton, was thrown principally with her brother Edward's children, on whom she bestowed the most constant affection. Cassandra was called after her mother, who had an only sister, Jane. Nearly three years after Cassandra's birth Mrs. Austen had the opportunity of giving the name of Jane to a newly born second daughter. She can little have imagined how familiar the name ' Jane Austen ' was to become in the course of the next century. Her father in a letter to a relation announces the arrival of another girl, who is to be called ' Jennie,' and who will be, he thinks, ' a present plaything for her sister Cassey and a future companion.' This prophecy was fully borne out in the life-long attachment of the two sisters : but Cassandra is by no means the only person to whom the author of ' Pride and Prejudice ' has proved to be a loved and honoured companion.

A very pleasant allusion to the family may be found in a paper contributed to the *National Review* (April 1907) by the Hon. Agnes Leigh and headed ' An Old Family History.' It consists of extracts from a manuscript record put together by one of the Leigh family (a first cousin of Mrs. George Austen)

in

---

[1] *Jane Austen's Sailor Brothers*, by J. H. and E. C. Hubback.

in 1788. Cassandra, she says, ' wife of the truly respectable Mr. Austen, has eight children—James, George,[1] Edward, Henry, Francis, Charles, Cassandra, and Jane. With his sons (all promising to make a figure in life) Mr. Austen educates a few youths of chosen friends and acquaintances. When among this family, the liberal society, the simplicity, hospitality, and taste, which commonly prevail in different families among the delightful valleys of Switzerland ever recur to my memory.'

Quiet and idyllic as this existence seems, the Austens touched the outside world at a sufficient number of points to enable the children to grow up with a greater knowledge of different phases of life than would usually be acquired in rectory houses at that date. George Austen's sister Philadelphia, after the death of her husband, Dr. Hancock, returned to Europe—but rather to Paris than to London. Her daughter Eliza was educated in Paris, went into French society, and married a Comte de Feuillide, who was guillotined in the French revolution. Eliza repaired to England when the troubles arose, and paid long visits to Steventon. ' She was a clever woman, and highly accomplished, after the French rather than the English mode,' who combined a somewhat restless love of society with a warm-hearted admiration for the family party at Steventon Rectory ; and it is evident that she took a leading part in the private theatricals which occasionally took place there. Eliza ended by marrying her cousin Henry.[2]

Another

---

[1] George was an invalid, who never appeared.

[2] *Memoir of Jane Austen* (by J. E. Austen Leigh), *and Lady Susan.* Richard Bentley and Son, 1871.

Another opening for varied society was provided by Mrs. Austen's brother, Mr. James Leigh Perrot, a rich and childless man who had a house at Bath as well as a place in Berkshire, and whose wife could easily introduce the girls to Bath coteries. Then two of the boys went to sea in a time of war, and must have kept the minds of the house party alive to the stirring events that were continually happening. It appears, also, that the usual English course of education for the two sexes was inverted in this family—the boys were brought up at home and not sent to school, while the girls got a good deal of teaching elsewhere. While Jane was still a young girl she had passed a year at Oxford under masters, she had gone through a course of similar studies at Southampton (where she had a fever of which she nearly died), and had afterwards gone with her sister to a school at Reading. If the subjects of her books are strictly confined to one sort of society, it was self-control rather than ignorance which dictated the limitation. In this united family the special pairs of brothers and sisters, both as to personal likeness and attachment, seem to have been Edward and Cassandra, Henry and Jane : though one might have thought that the humour and love of fun which either possessed would have brought Edward and Jane specially near to each other. But Henry also had humour in his composition. ' His letter to me,' writes Jane, ' was most affectionate and kind as well as entertaining : there is no merit in him in *that*, he cannot help being amusing.' Henry indeed must have possessed an almost exasperating buoyancy and sanguineness of temperament and high animal spirits

spirits which no misfortunes could depress and no failures damp.

But no attachment of brother to sister could equal that which existed between Cassandra and Jane.[1]   It was character-ised on the part of Jane by an almost deferential affection which never diminished in respectfulness as she grew older and more famous ; and on the part of Cassandra by an admiration entirely devoid of jealousy.   Each opened her mind to the other in a manner very imperfectly appreciated by those who rely only on their published correspondence. Cassandra was so much impressed by the sacredness of this correspondence that she destroyed all the letters in which special emotion had been shown, and felt sure she had left only what no one would care to publish.   We believe that some involuntary injustice has been done to Jane's character, even by her particular admirers, from their not having properly appreciated the imperfection of the record.

We have also to remember that, apart from these letters, nearly all our reminiscences of her (valuable as they are to us) come from a nephew and nieces who belonged to a different generation, and were not, after all, likely to be the recipients of her most intimate confidences.   One of these nieces, however, after describing her playfulness and fun, and adding that she never played with life's serious responsibilities, says, ' When grave, she was *very* grave ; I am not sure but that Aunt Cassandra's

---

[1] The paragraphs relating to Jane Austen are based partly on published books (especially the Memoir by the Rev. J. E. Austen Leigh and the Correspondence edited by Lord Brabourne) and partly on unpublished family records.

Cassandra's disposition was not the more equally cheerful of the two.' There were depths in the quiet, self-contained nature of the author which were not easily fathomed ; and the idea that she was in any way deficient in emotional consciousness (though they would not have used that phrase) would have been scouted by all her family as preposterous.

But it is evident that Jane Austen deliberately suppressed a part of herself in her writings, in order to concentrate her whole force on the particular ends to which it was directed. For instance, it is the universal testimony of her nephews and nieces that she was especially well suited for intercourse with children. 'Aunt Jane was the general favourite with children, her ways with them being so playful.' 'She seemed to love you, and you loved her naturally in return.' Yet the sentimental aspect of childhood, of which some of her successors have made so much, never appears in her books. Then again she had such a love for natural scenery that she would sometimes say that she thought it must form one of the delights of heaven ; but she seldom allowed herself to introduce descriptions of it into her books, although one or two pictures, such as the summer view from the terrace at Donwell, autumn in the hedgerows of Uppercross, the dancing sea at Portsmouth, and the varied beauties of Lyme, show what she might have made of it. Again, we cannot for a moment doubt that, as we have already said, hers was an emotional nature, capable of deep feeling. Yet she was determined that the humorous and the cheerful should prevail in her writings, the romantic only cropping up at intervals : although the closing scenes of 'Persuasion' might

have

have proved, had she lived, the introduction to a different province of fiction.

In the year 1801 Mr. Austen resigned the care of the parish of Steventon to his son James—his eventual successor in the benefice—and retired with his wife and daughters to Bath, where no doubt many other retired clergymen congregated, and where they might from time to time see Mrs. Austen's brother, Mr. Leigh Perrot, and his wife. There Mr. Austen died in 1805, and in the next year his widow, with Cassandra and Jane, took up her quarters for a time at Southampton. In 1808 Edward Austen was able to offer a choice of homes to his mother and sisters, who had now been joined by their friend Miss Martha Lloyd, sister of Mrs. James Austen. The ladies chose the cottage at Chawton, which has been already mentioned.

'Everybody,' writes Jane Austen from Southampton, 'is very much concerned at our going away, and everybody is acquainted with Chawton and speaks of it as a remarkably pretty village, and everybody knows the house we describe, but nobody fixes on the right.'

Mrs. Knight (now living at Canterbury) must have suggested an inference from the fact that the Rector of Chawton had no wife, for Jane proceeds : ' I am very much obliged to Mrs. Knight for such proof of the interest she takes in me, and she may depend upon it that I *will* marry Mr. Papillon, whatever may be his reluctance, or my own ; I owe her much more than such a trifling sacrifice ! ' This idea must have survived as a family joke for some years. Much later she writes to a nephew : ' I am happy to tell you that Mr. Papillon will

Jane Austen

Emery Walker Ph.sc.

will soon make his offer, probably next Monday, as he returns on Saturday. His *intention* can no longer be doubtful in the smallest degree, as he has secured the refusal of the house which Mrs. Baverstock at present occupies in Chawton, and is to vacate soon, which of course is intended for Mrs. Elizabeth Papillon'; this lady being the Rector's maiden sister.

Mr. Papillon, or anyone else, might well have been charmed by the appearance and bearing of a person who could be described, as Jane was by one of her nieces, in the following terms : ' the Figure tall and slight, but not drooping ; well-balanced, as was proved by her quick firm step. Her complexion of that rather rare sort which seems the peculiar property of *light brunettes*; a mottled skin, not fair, but perfectly clear and healthy in hue ; the fine naturally curling hair, neither light nor dark ; the bright hazel eyes to match, and the rather small but well-shaped nose.'

Edward was only an occasional resident at Chawton. Godmersham was his home by preference, and there his relations were always sure of a kind welcome. One year, however, when he was painting the house at Godmersham, he spent five months at Chawton, to the great pleasure of his mother and sisters. Jane writes to her brother Frank (July 1813) : ' We go on in the most comfortable way, very frequently dining together, and always meeting in some part of every day. Edward is very well, and enjoys himself as thoroughly as any Hampshire-born Austen can desire. Chawton is not thrown away on him.' [1]

At

---

[1] *Jane Austen's Sailor Brothers.*

At Chawton the sisters were within reach of their brother James at Steventon, and Edward often lent the 'Great House,' as it was then called, to one or other of his sailor brothers.

These, then, were the home and surroundings of Jane Austen, during the last and most fruitful period of her literary career. She had indeed, as readers of her biography know, entered on the career of authoress as a child ; she had in fact written more and read less in youth than her mature judgment could approve. In the early years of her womanhood she had composed at all events the first drafts of three of the six novels on which her fame rests ; and one of them, 'Northanger Abbey,' was complete enough to be sold to a publisher, who after all declined to publish. Then follow six or eight years of almost absolute silence. Shortly before the beginning of this period occurred, probably, the one romance of her life. We have it on the authority of her sister that about that time Jane met in the West of England a young man between whom and herself was formed a mutual bond of attachment, soon to be snapped asunder by his death. Perhaps this event, added to the disappointment about 'Northanger Abbey,' the death of her father, and the unsettlement of her home, are enough to account for her disuse of the pen. At all events she resumed its employment when she settled at Chawton, and never laid it down again until she was too weak to hold it.

The ladies began their residence at the Cottage in July 1809 ; and we are told that Jane occupied her first year there in preparing 'Sense and Sensibility' and 'Pride and Prejudice' for publication. Probably we must extend this work over a longer period, for she did not begin 'Mansfield Park'

Park' until February 1811. 'Sense and Sensibility' must have received almost its final polish by that time, for it was actually published in October 1811, while 'Pride and Prejudice' did not follow until January 1813. It is possible that this interval gave time for a more complete revision of the latter work, as its greater perfection and

WEDGWOOD SOUP TUREEN, CHOSEN FOR GODMERSHAM, SEPT. 1813
(*Jane Austen's Letters*, vol. ii. p. 158.)

maturity would lead us to expect. By the time of its publication the author was far advanced with 'Mansfield Park,' and 'Emma' followed in due course.

The party of ladies at the Cottage lived, however, so retired a life, that it must have been principally in London with Henry, or at Godmersham with Edward, that Jane was able

to

to add a mature observation of the varieties of human nature to her youthful studies in that direction at Bath and elsewhere. Something, however, she could do (like her own Elizabeth Bennett) in the narrow circle round her by noting the ever-changing dispositions of her neighbours ; and even if they proved uninteresting, she had at least the satisfaction of comparing them with the creations of her own imagination. ' As soon as a whist party was formed,' she says, fresh from the composition of ' Mansfield Park,' ' I made my mother an excuse and came away, leaving just as many for *their* round table as there were at Mrs. Grant's. I wish they might be as agreeable a set.' She could always extract enjoyment and amusement from very quiet surroundings. ' To sit in idleness,' she says, ' over a good fire in a well-proportioned room is a luxurious sensation. Sometimes we talked and sometimes we were quite silent : I said two or three amusing things and Mr. H. made a few infamous puns.'

In a letter written before she left Southampton, Jane, after contrasting her advanced age of thirty-three with her own girlhood, adds : ' I felt with thankfulness that I was quite as happy now as then.' On the whole, it is probable that the first six years of her residence at Chawton were as happy as any part of her life. She was among her own people, and in a comfortable, though modest, home ; she had the engrossing occupation of authorship, and the pleasure of a slowly growing fame. But the last year or two of her life were saddened by failing health and overclouded by family anxieties and disappointments. In March 1816 the bankruptcy of her favourite brother Henry was announced.

announced. The failure of a bank at Alton which his London bank had supported contributed largely to this calamity. No personal extravagance was charged against him, but he had the mortification of feeling that he had embarrassed several of his nearest relations (who had been acting as his sureties) by his failure. Among others his brother Edward lost the large sum of £20,000. Nor was this Edward's only money trouble at the time. He had been threatened for two or three years with the loss of all his Hampshire property. Some informality in a disentailing deed executed in 1755 was alleged to have been discovered. The result would apparently have been that the instrument remained good as long as the Brodnax line (for they had executed it) survived, but that on their failing the heirs-at-law of Elizabeth Knight came in. Such heirs-at-law there were. They did not all want to assert their claim, but some of the Baverstocks and Hintons did so. The affair dragged on several years, and was finally compromised by Edward Knight paying the large sum of £15,000. 'This it was, I believe,' writes a niece, about half a century later, 'that occasioned the great gap in Chawton Park Wood, visible for 30 years afterwards, and probably not filled up again even now.'

The gradual shrinkage in the party of ladies at Chawton Cottage has already been mentioned. We need only add that after the death of Cassandra Austen in 1845 the Cottage was used for labourers' tenements, and that the main part of it has now for some years been occupied as a village club.

Meanwhile, in 1826, the squire's eldest son, Edward (who had been High Sheriff of Hants in 1823), took up his residence

at

at Chawton House, which has never again been without its regular occupants.

The squire himself lived on at Godmersham until his death, which took place 19th November 1852. He had been able to take his usual drive on the preceding day ; early in the morning of the 19th he desired his servant to leave him, as he felt comfortable and should go to sleep. He seemed to be asleep when the servant returned, but it was the sleep of death. ' It strikes me,' wrote one of his relations soon afterwards, ' as a characteristic end of his prosperous and placid life, and he will certainly leave on the minds of all who knew him an image of Gentleness and quiet Cheerfulness of no ordinary degree.'

He left a large family of sons and daughters, and many of his descendants are now living. His six sons were all educated at Winchester School. George, the second son, married, but died without issue. Henry was in the 9th Lancers, was twice married, and left issue by both his wives. William was for many years Rector of Steventon, occupying there a new rectory house built to replace the house which had so long been the home of his grandfather and uncle. He married as his first wife Caroline Portal, and left issue by her. He married a second and a third time, but left no further issue. Charles, Rector of Chawton, never married, and John, who was in the Carabineers, married, but left no issue.

Of the daughters, Fanny, the eldest, the devoted friend of her aunt Jane, was wife of Sir Edward Knatchbull, and mother of the first Lord Brabourne ; and Elizabeth, who married Mr. Rice of Danecourt, has left numerous descendants. So has Cassandra, who married Lord George Hill.

We return to the eldest son, Edward, whom we have seen
settled

After a painting by Sir Francis Grant P.R.A.

Emery Walker Ph.sc.

Edwd Knight

settled at Chawton. He married, first, in May 1826, Mary Dorothea, daughter of Sir Edward Knatchbull, Bart., who died in 1838 ; and secondly, in March 1840, Adela, daughter of John Portal, Esq., of Freefolk Priors, Hants, and he has left issue by both marriages.

CAKE BASKET BY PAUL LAMERIE

Mr. Knight's residence at Chawton, which began in 1826, lasted for the remainder of his life. He transferred his allegiance from Kent to Hants, and never moved to Godmersham, finally severing his connexion with that place by selling the bulk of his property there in 1874. He took an active part in local and county business, and a deep interest in his Hampshire home ; improving the house by the addition of a billiard-room and more commodious offices. His portrait by Sir
Francis

Francis Grant, given to his wife in 1864 by his friends and neighbours, is a proof of the estimation in which he was held, and an ocular demonstration of the handsome features which he inherited from his parents. Some of his principal characteristics are shown in the following sentences taken from a notice in the *Hampshire Chronicle* at the time of his death in 1879: 'An intelligent and keen sportsman and an unrivalled horseman, he will long be remembered by those who had the pleasure of following him when he hunted with the celebrated H. H. Hounds. He was the principal founder and President of the N.E. Hants Agricultural Association which owes its prosperity greatly to the active interest he took in its management. All who have attended the annual dinners of the Society must have remarked the spontaneous heartiness with which the toast of his health was always met by the members, and how the song of "The Fine old English Gentleman" followed with singular appropriateness. His great courtesy, his dignified bearing, his invariable and hearty kindness and good temper and above all his remarkable uprightness and appreciation of honour, truth, and duty, secured him a position not often equalled in the respect and love of all who had the advantage of his acquaintance. Openhearted, hospitable, and generous, endowed with considerable abilities, and a good sense which seldom failed him, a staunch and loyal friend, unswerving in the support of whatever he believed to be right, and just, and incapable of anything that even savoured of meanness or deception he worthily discharged the duties of a country gentleman.'

With his death we close this history.

APPENDICES

APPENDIX I

Grant of Land, 14th of Edward II

Know all present and to come That we John de St John have given granted and by this our present charter confirmed to Hugh Byne of Chautone four acres of arable land in Chautone one end of which extends towards Mundchamesrude on the west and the other extends towards the common lands of the town of Chautone on the East and abuts on the highway by the Pass of Aultone towards the North and on the other side on the wood of Richard Pyngel towards the South To have hold and enclose the aforesaid four acres of land with the appurtenances of us and our heirs by the aforesaid Hugh Byne his heirs and assigns freely quietly well and in peace for ever the aforesaid Hugh Byne his heirs and assigns paying therefor to us and our heirs sixpence per annum payable at the four principal terms of the year in equal portions for all other services actions and demands   And we the aforesaid John de St John and our heirs will warrant acquit and for ever defend against all people the aforesaid four acres of land and appurtenances to the aforesaid Hugh Byne his heirs and assigns   In witness whereof we have affixed our seal to this present charter Given at Halnakede . . . the Feast of St Mathew the Apostle in the fourteenth year of the Reign of King Edward the son of King Edward   These being witnesses, Robert de Tystede, Henry de Estone, William Gervays, William de Rutherfeld, Roger Dalron, William de Mundham, John atte Streyte, and many others.

Grant of Land 17th of Edward II

SCIANT present and to come   That I Luke atte Oke of Chawton have given granted and by this my present CHARTER have confirmed to John Wyn of Cicester for a certain sum of money which he gave to me in hand my one messuage and ten acres of land with their appurtenances in the village of Chauton whereof the aforesaid messuage is situated between the messuage of Richard Tilye on the one part and the messuage of Cecilia Golleghe on the other part And one acre of land lies at Kacre between the land of Roger Dalron and certain land formerly of Mathew le Harpour And one half acre lies there in the same culture between the land of John atte Streyte and the land of Adam le Pye And one half acre lies at La Estforlonge between the land of Roger Dalron and Hugh Byene And one half acre in the same culture between the land of Richard Shepherd on either side   And one half acre lies in the same culture between the land of Robert Andrew and abuts at one end on the meadow of Walter Faber of Chauton and one half acre lies at Holebrouke between the land of Richard Tilye and Roger Dalron And one acre of land lies at La Shottelonde between the land of Robert Pugeys and the land of Nicholas le Hackar and one half acre lies in the same culture between the land of Richard Shepherd and the land of Robert Andrew And one half acre in the same culture between the land of the Lord Rector of Chauton and the land of Nicholas le Hackar And one acre lies at la Merslade between (the land) of Richard Tilie and the land of Nicholas le Hackar And one half acre of land which is Forhalue lies next a certain culture of land of Roger Dalron And one half acre lies next Le Paas between the land of the Chaplain of the Chapel of Chauton and the land of John le Knyght And one half acre lies in La Dene between the land of Roger Dalron and the land of Walter Smith And one rood of land lies next Le Paas between the land formerly Mathew le Harpours And one rood lies at La Crockelonde between the land of the Lord Rector of Chauton and the land of Roger Dalron And one half acre lies in the same culture between the land

of

of Richard Shepherd and the land of Hugh Byene And one acre lies next the close of the Lord Rector of Chauton between the land of Hugh Byene on either side To have and to hold the aforesaid messuage and ten acres of land with all their appurtenances together with all lands and tenements which in any manner may further fall to me or my heirs of the cheif lord of that fee to the aforesaid John Wyn and his heirs or assigns freely quietly and in peace justly in inheritance for ever the aforesaid John his heirs or assigns rendering and doing therefor annually to the cheif lord for that fee the rents and services thereof due and accustomed And I the said Luke and my heirs or assigns will warrant acquit and securely defend for ever against all people the aforesaid messuage and ten acres of land with all their appurtenances together with all the lands and tenements which may or ought in any wise further fall to me or my heirs by the aforesaid rents and services to be paid and done to the chief lord of that fee

IN WITNESS whereof I have confirmed this charter with the impression of my seal These being witnesses Thomas le Marays then Steward of Lord John de Sᵗ John, Roger Dalron, Hugh Byene, Walter Faber, John le Knyght, Robert Pugeys, Nicholas le Hackare, Richard Pyngel, Thomas Thurbirn of Basings Clerk Notary of this Charter, and many others Given at Chauton on the Sunday next after the feast of the Translation of Sᵗ Thomas the Martyr in the beginning of the seventeenth year of the Reign of King Edward son of King Edward.

APPENDIX II

THE following are some of the ancient names of fields to be found in the Court Rolls and ancient charters, the majority of which cannot now be identified.

Keynes.
Carpenters.
Hobandrews (adjoining Chawton Cottage and Siblets).
Castelland.

Arrow

Arrow Croft.
Hurlebatts, now Hulvers.
Archers, now Orchards.
Scatwinch Close.
Northern Brooks, now Norton Brooks.
Southern Brooks, now Sutton Brooks.
Scattenns.
Sheepemead.
Mundchamesrude (John de St. John to Hugh Byne, 14th Edw. II).
Merschslade   (13th Edw. III).
Mulclhynch   ,,   ,,
Twyne Street   ,,   ,,   Winstreet.
Estfurlong   (17th Edw. II) Ashfurlong.
La Holebrouke   ,,   ,,   Holebrook.
La Merslade   ,,   ,,
La Dene   ,,   ,,
La Paas   ,,   ,,
The Pass of Aulton (22nd Edw. III).
Andrewes Lane (28th Edw. III).
Le Rigge (1st Edw. IV), The Ridge.
Lamvalslond (5th Hen. V).
Wheelers (Ct. Roll 12th April ; 16th Hen. VIII).
Westfield (6th Edw. II).

Chawton Common Fields [1]

	A.	R.	P.
The acreage of the common fields was	309	0	32
and of the Common	321	0	5

The names and extent of the common fields were :

	A.	R.	P.
South Field	83	2	28
North Field	38	2	5
Ridge Field	19	3	13
White Down	33	3	23
Winstreet	9	0	1
Upper East Field	78	0	11
Lower East Field	46	0	31

South

[1] See Appendix IX.

South Field included South Field and the plat ; Lower Yew Tree Piece ; the Glebe, Southfield ; about 14 acres of the Glebe meadow behind the Rectory adjoining South Field ; and the Stripp of Land containing 28½ acres adjoining the road called the Shrave from the way to Inbrook Wood to the end of Hatchgates —except Beans Close—*2a. 2r. 10p.*

North Field included the four North Fields from the Shrave to the Pace way or common except the upper part of middle North Field—not including Peaseway or Paceway Close.

Ridge Field was much the same as the present Ridge Field now divided by the new Meon Valley Line.

White Down abutted on Ackender Wood, White Down Lane and the Road from Alton to Alresford.

Winstreet lay between the two roads leading to the Butts or Robin Hood Butts, as they were then called.

Upper East Field included Mingledown, Mounters East Field, and the other East Fields, and Great and Little Maslets.

Lower East Field included old Brook Vere, Style Piece and Great Field.

APPENDIX III

RECTORS OF CHAWTON

Instituted.	Name.	Vacated.	Patron.
	William Wanbridge	res'd 1289	
4 Oct. 1289	Thomas St. John		Sir John St. John
16 Aug. 1315	Walter Champeneys		Sir John St. John
27 Dec. 1333	Hugh Gylle	died 1342	Hugh St. John
20 April 1342	John Scharp	res'd 1342	Sir William Trussel, guardian of Hugh St. John
16 Dec. 1342	Richard de Wystone		Do.
18 Sept. 1343	Thomas de Saxlingham	died 1346	Thos. de Arpale
1 Aug. 1346	John de Broughtone		Henry Moyne, on behalf of William Trussel
			5 Oct. 1351

Instituted.	Name.	Vacated.	Patron.
5 Oct. 1351	John Beel		Walter de Heyward and Henry Forester, R. of Eton. Proxies for John de St. Philibert
8 Sept. 1361	John de Eytone	died 1372	Thos. de Aldingham, in right of his wife Margaret, dau. of Hugh St. John
26 Sept. 1372	Walter de Donwyche		Sir Luke de Ponynges
14 June 1390	Henry Prout		Sir Thos. Wortynge
	Thos. Alwyn	res'd 1453	
13 July 1453	John Hamonde	res'd 1460	Godfrey Hylton
5 July 1460	William Preston	res'd 1466	Elinor St. John, widow
23 Jan. 1466	John Elyot	died 1486	John Bonvyle
20 Aug. 1486	John Turpyn	died 1514	John Bonvyle
20 May 1514	Richard Shelstone	res'd 1532	John Shelstone, in right of concession by Florence Fulford, dau. of John Bonvyle
4 April 1532	Thomas Wemme	died 1551	Sir Thos. West Ld La Warr and Elizabeth his wife
11 July 1551	John White		Do.
20 April 1553	Wm. Darrell		
23 June 1554	Arthur Elmer		
	Justinian Lancaster		Henry Kingston de Chawton hac vice by assignment of Wm. Apsley of Poynings, exor. of John Lloyd the true Patron, in virtue of the assignment of the advowson by Thos. West Lord La Warr
11 Oct. 1574	Thomas Bylson		Queen Elizabeth
6 Sept. 1578	John Lawrence		Collated by the Bishop 21 June 1582

Instituted.	Name.	Vacated.	Patron.
21 June 1582	John Constantine		
30 Nov. 1583	Thomas Nevill		
	John Tilborow	died 1600	
17 Feb. 1600–1	John Barlow	died 1601	John Knight
21 July 1601	Nicholas Love		John Knight
	Richard Mason		John Knight
23 March 1614	John Blythman	died 1634	John Knight
21 Nov. 1634	James Sessions		The King ' ratione lunaciæ Johan Knight '
23 Sept. 1662	Henry Bradshaw		Sir Richard Knight
27 Sept. 1690	Colwell Brickenden		Christopher Knight
14 May 1714	William Lloyd		William Knight
24 Jan. 1718	John Baker		William Knight
15 June 1742	Henry Haddon		Thomas Knight
28 March 1744	John Hinton	died 1802	Thomas Knight
1 Oct. 1802	John Rawston Papillon		William Deedes and Lewis Cage, trustees of Edward Knight
24 May 1837	Charles Bridges Knight	died 1867	Edward Knight
6 Feb. 1868	Edward Bridges Knight	res'd 1876	Edward Knight
24 July 1876	Charles Edward Knight		Edward Knight

APPENDIX IV

THE following is a complete record of the remaining inscriptions contained in Chawton Church, other than those described in the text. On the north wall of the Chancel are (1) a black and white marble tablet, inscribed as follows :—

Sacred to the Memory of
The REV'D CHARLES BRIDGES KNIGHT,
Fifth son of Edward Knight
of Godmersham Park, Kent
and Chawton House, Hants.
Esquire,
He was Rector of this Parish
for 30 years,
and died Oct. 13th, 1867,
Aged 64.
Deservedly beloved and deeply regretted
by all who knew him.

The Lord shall be unto thee
an everlasting Light and thy
God thy Glory. Is. 60. xix.

(2) A brass within a black marble frame (engraved on it the arms impaling Pearson) inscribed :—

In Memory of JOHN BROOK KNIGHT
late Captain in the 6th Dragoon Guards, Carabineers,
youngest son of Edward Knight of Godmersham
Park Kent and Chawton House. Esq're
Died January 10th 1878 aged 69.

Looking unto Jesus.

On

On the north wall within the Altar rails is a monument to Elizabeth Knight with this inscription :—

In the Vault near this place
ELI: KNIGHT WID. only daughter of Michael Martin
of Ensom^e in Oxfordsh. Gent. by Frances youngest
daughter of Sir Christ. Lewknor of West Dean in Sussex
Esq. She married to her first husband William
Woodward of Fosters in Surry Esqre who died Oct^r
26th 1721 And to her second husband Bulstrode Peachey
of Petworth in Sussex Esqre who died 14 Jan. 1735.
They both took the name of Knight upon their marriage.

On the south side of the Altar is a black and white marble monument with semi-recumbent effigy to Sir Richard Knight, dating from 1679, with the arms, crest and motto. The inscription is as follows :—

H. S. E.
RICHARDUS KNIGHT Miles hujus Comitatus
Vice-Præfectus regius, Tribunus Peditum Equitum Capitaneus
magnis illis muneribus egregie functus
pluribus et majoribus idoneus
Varios exterorum mores peregre proficiscendo perspexerat
patrios ex animo probavit
Omnis elegantiæ cultor eximius, idem omnis exemplar
peritissimorum Artificum Altor et Fautor,
maxime munificentia, Ingenio magis
Cum Eruditis Consuetudinem cum Ingenuis Dignitatem, cum optimis
Amicitiam instituit, ornavit, coluit
Novis honoribus assignatus decretæ Provinciæ gloriam ipse reportavit
Tumultum et Invidiam aliis reliquit
Ferventibusque jam tum Comitiis
Spem Populi, Cleri desiderium, Optimatum Delicias
Una secum abstulit An° D^ni MDCLXXIX. Æt. XL.

Above

Above the figures on this monument is this incription :—

H. S. E.
CHRISTOPHER KNIGHT, Armiger, MICHAELIS MARTIN,
de Ensham in Comitat. Oxon.
Generosi Filius nec non
Richardi Knight Militis hæres
et Re et Virtute
Majus quod merita vindicent
Ejus dum apud vivos agebat
Sæpius prohibuit Verecundia
Eulogium.
Ob^t Londini mens. Octob. die vigesimo secundo
Anno Dom. MDCCII
Ætatis suæ
33

There is also a black marble slab on the floor in front of the Altar. The arms are quarterly Martin and Lewkenor with a wyvern for the crest, thus inscribed :—

H. S. E.
CHRISTOPHERUS KNIGHT Armiger
ob^t mens. Octob. die 22do
AD. MDCCII ætat.
33
Cujus fratris amicissimi
piæ memoriæ
Soror Dna Elizabetha Knight
hoc saxum
ob luctum ipsa prope saxum
sacrum jubet

On

On the south wall is a black and white marble tablet :—

In Memory of
CATHERINE ANN,
second daughter of the late
William Prowting, Esq.,
of this Parish
She died Mar. 17th. 1848
aged 65
and was interred in the family Vault
in the Church yard.

The souls of the Righteous are in the hand of God.
Wisdom. III chap. 1 verse.

Next comes a brass :—

In Memory of
BENJAMIN CLEMENT, Captain R.N.
who died Nov. 5th AD. 1835 aged 50
and of
ANN MARY his wife
youngest daughter of
William Prowting of this Parish Esquire
Died Aug. 30th. 1858. aged 70
also of their sons
WILLIAM THOMAS
died January 13th. 1864 aged 43
and
BENJAMIN PROWTING, M.A.
of Exeter College, Oxford,
34 years Minor Canon of the Cathedral Church
of Winchester.
Died Nov'r 27th. 1873. aged 60

R. I. P.

In

2 B

In Memory of
WILLIAM PROWTING of Chawton
Justice of the Peace & Deputy Lieutenant for this County
who died June 24th. AD. 1821 aged 67
and of
ELIZABETH his wife
who died Sept. 2nd. 1832. aged 80
also of their sons
WILLIAM died June 19th. 1799 aged 14
JOHN ROWLAND died June 14th. 1800 aged 9
R. I. P.

The family vault is at the south-east corner of the Churchyard.
On the walls of the Vestry are two marble tablets, one in memory
of Mrs. George Austen, the other of her daughter Cassandra Eliza-
beth. Two of Mrs. Austen's children, viz. her eldest son James
(Rector of Steventon after his father) and her younger daughter
Jane (the novelist), had predeceased her.
The inscriptions are as follows :—

In Memory of
CASSANDRA AUSTEN
daughter of the late
Reverend Thomas Leigh,
Rector of Harpsden—Oxfordshire,
and relict of the late
Reverend George Austen
Rector of Steventon Hants,
She died the 18th day of Jan'y 1827
Aged 87 years.
Leaving four sons
and one daughter surviving, namely
Edward Knight
of Chawton House in this Parish
Henry Thomas Austen
Francis William Austen

Charles

Charles John Austen
Cassandra Elizabeth Austen
who have inscribed this tablet
to the Memory of
an affectionate and beloved parent.

In Memory of
CASSANDRA ELIZABETH
AUSTEN
daughter of the late
Reverend George Austen,
Rector of Steventon
in this County.
Died 22nd. March 1845. Aged 72.
Being justified by Faith we have peace with
God through our Lord Jesus Christ.
Rom. V. I.

On the north wall of the aisle are two tablets to the Hinton
family :—
In the Churchyard near this spot lie the
remains of the
REVEREND JOHN HINTON
During fifty eight years. Rector of this Parish who
died Ap'l 11th. 1802. aged 82.
He passed his life amongst his flock in the discharge
of every duty,
exhibiting a singular and most exemplary pattern of
the Christian Character.
Near the same place are interred MARTHA his first wife
only surviving child of the Reverend Edward Hinton
Rector of Sheering in Essex who died July 1761 and
JANE his second wife, daughter of Thomas Harrison
of Alton—who died Ap'l 15th. 1799.
This tribute is to their memory inscribed by their
affectionate children.

In

In Memory of
THE REV'D JAMES VENTRIS D.D.
Vicar of Beeding in Sussex
who died 31st January 1841 aged 80 years
and of JANE his wife daughter of the late
Rev'd John Hinton M.A. Rector of this Parish
She died 31st December 1856 aged 85.

Also of her Brother JOHN HINTON Esq
who died 26th Ap'l 1846 at Otterbourne
in this county aged 72
Blessed are the dead,
Which die in the Lord.

Adjoining these two is a tablet in memory of the first wife of Edward Knight and their eldest son. This was formerly fixed against the Chancel wall, but was removed to its present position on the rebuilding of the Church after the fire.

In the vault beneath are deposited the remains of
MARY DOROTHEA wife of Edward Knight Esq.,
Of Chawton House, in this Parish,
and eldest daughter of the Rt. Hon. Sir Edward Knatchbull Bart
of Mersham Hatch, in the county of Kent,
She died in London, on the 22nd day of February, 1838
In the 31st year of her age.
Leaving issue five sons & two daughters,
Her afflicted husband caused this Tablet to be erected
To record his irreparable loss,
And in the hope that her children when they read these lines
May call to mind and endeavour to imitate the virtues
of a good and affectionate Mother.
In the same sacred place are laid the remains of her eldest son
EDWARD LEWKENOR,
who died at Tunbridge Wells on the 19th day of May 1838
Aged 11 years.

The Lord gave and the Lord hath taken away,
Blessed be the name of the Lord.

The

The monument to William Knight was removed to its present position from the Chancel when the Church was rebuilt in 1871. It formerly stood where the organ now is.

Near this place
Lyes the body of WILLIAM WOODWARD KNIGHT
Esq'r (the only son of Edward Woodward Esq're
of Fosters in Surrey by Elizabeth the eldest
Daughter & Coheir to Sir Christopher
Lewkenor of West Dean Sussex) who
assumed the name of Knight upon his
Marriage to Elizabeth the only daughter
of Michael Martin Gent: of Ensome in
Oxfordshire (whose Mother was a Knight
and heir to Sir Richard Knight of this place)
by Frances the other Coheir to the s'd Sr.
Christopher Lewkenor, whereby were
united the several Estates of the Lewkenors,
Knights, Woodwards & Martins.
A Gentleman
Dutiful to his God, True to his Country, Affectionate to his wife, sincere to his Friend, Charitable and obliging to all. He died Member of Parliament for Midhurst, Sussex, Oct'r 26, 1721. To his memory this monument was erected by his disconsolate Relict. A.D. 1723.

In Memory of
WILLIAM LEE-JORTIN, Esq.,
who died at Woolley Lodge, Berks.
August 8th. 1861 aged 54 years
He was the second son of Richard E. N. Lee Esq. by
Elizabeth daughter of William Prowting Esq. of this Parish,
and in 1844 on succeeding to the property of his relative
John Jortin Esq of Nibley House in the County of Gloucester
assumed by Royal Sign Manual the additional surname of Jortin.
We must through much tribulation enter into the Kingdom of God,
Acts. XIV. 22.
Sacred

Sacred
To the Memory
of
CHARLES ERNEST KNIGHT
Captain in the 77th. Regiment,
Fourth son of Edward Knight Esq.,
of Chawton House in ths Parish,
and Mary Dorothea his wife
Born in London Oct. 13th. 1836
Educated at Harrow
and the R. M. C. Sandhurst,
he joined his Regiment in the Crimea,
in November 1854
and after distinguishing himself
by his gallant conduct before the enemy
on several occasions,
and especially at the attack
on the Rifle Pits
on the night of the 19th of Ap'l 1855
He fell ill of fever shortly after
the taking of Sebastopol
on the 8th of September,
and died in Camp on Oct. 2nd. 1855
His many amiable qualities endeared him
to the officers and men of his Regiment,
and while the premature close of a life,
so full of promise,
cannot but cause deep sorrow
to his Family,
Yet are they able to resign him,
to the will of that Lord in whom,
as they humbly believe, he fell asleep.

He is numbered among the children of God,
And his lot is among the Saints.

Wis. CV. v. 5.

In

In Memory of
HERBERT LEWKENOR born at Chawton, Sept. 26th. 1873,
Died at Khairwarra, Rajpootana, Mar. 19th. 1874
Also of
DARYL COLBORNE born at Lucknow Jan. 25th. 1872
Died at Odeypore. May 30th. 1874
Infant sons of Major Bradford and Elizabeth Adela
his wife, dau. of Edward Knight of Chawton House.

The Lord hath need of them.

To the Glory of God
and in Memory of his faithful Servants
GEORGE WOLFE,
who died Sept. 20th. 1883, aged 49
and of
ANNE MARY his wife
only daughter of Captain Benjamin Clement R.N.
who died February 22nd. 1893. Aged 69.
R. I. P.

This brass is erected in memory by their neice,
Lilias Edith Clement.

To the Glory of God
and in loving Memory of
WILLIAM THOMAS CLEMENT,
youngest son of Captain Benjamin Clement, R.N.
who died January 13th. 1864 aged 43
and of
LILIAS EDITH CLEMENT,
his only daughter,
who died Feb'y 2nd. 1895 aged 35.

R. I. P.

APPENDIX V

Probate of the Will of JOHN KNIGHT THE ELDER.

Prerogative Court of Canterbury

John Knight,   Reg :
  Senr   Chawnay fo. 48.

IN the Name of God Amen, the xxviiith daye of September In the yere of O^r Lorde God a thousande five hundred fiftie and nine.

I John Knyght Senr of the Parrish of Chawton in the Countie of South: and within the dioc^s of Winchester being hole of mynde and of good and perfecte remembrance albeit weake and sicke in bodie, lawde and prayse be unto Allmightie God Do constitute and ordayne this my present Testament contayning herein my last will and mynde in maner and forme followinge, that is to say, First and principallie I comend and bequeath my soule to Allmighty Jesu my maker and redemer in whome and by the merrite of whose blessed passion is all my whole truste of there remission and forgiveness of all my sinnes and my bodie to be buried in my parrish Church of Chawton aforsayed Item I give and bequeath to the Mother Church of Saynte Trynyte in Winchester xii*d*. Item I give and bequeath to the Highe Alter of my pishe Church for my oblacōns and tithes necligentlie forgotten or withdrawne in discharge of my conscience xii*d*.   Item I give and bequeath toward the reparacōns of my parrishe Church xxs.   Item I give and bequeath to John Knight my brother Richard Knight's son xxs.   Item I give and bequeath to Davie Knight my kinsman vi shepe.   Item I give and bequeath to the reste of my brother Richard's children everie one of them ii*d*. a piece   Item I give and bequeath to everie Godchilde that I have vi*d*. a piece   Item I give and bequeath to everie servante that I have in my howse xii*d*. a piece   Item I bequeath to everie poore householder in Chawton aforesayed xii*d*.   Item I give and bequeath to Jone my wife xx^{li} of myn owne propper goods and her owne apparell that she hathe and her owne goods that she brought to me which is exprest in an Inventory.   Item if my wiffe be with childe I will and give it xx^{li} to be payed if it be a woman

childe

childe at the day of her marriage or at the age of xxiii yeres, if it be a manchild to be delivered at thage of xxi yeres and if it fortune to departe the worlde and not lyve untill it be come to the age aforesaide Then I will that the said xx^{li} shall remayne unto Harry Knighte my sonne. The residue of all my goods and lands tenements wastes pastures medowes grounds woods commons rents reversions and service withall and singular the appurtenances which I the sayed John have sett lyinge and beinge within the parish of Chawton or ellswhere within the Countie of South: with all my goods moveable and immoveable not given nor bequeathed my debts payed and my legaces fulfilled I give it all frelie to Harry Knyght my sonne whome I ordayne and make to be my full and hole executor And he to see my debts payed and my legacies fulfilled Item I ordaine and make to be my Overseers of this my laste Will and Testament Sir Thomas White whome for his oversight and counsell towards my sonne I give xl*s*. with John Knight my brother and Lawrence Mathew and they to have for theire labore and paynestakinge xx*s*.

I bequeath to the mending of the highe waye x*s*.

Proved at London 19 Oct. 1559 by Henry Knight, Executor.

EXTRACTS FROM THE WILL OF NICHOLAS KNIGHT

Will proved 8th February 1583. P.C. Canterbury.

Nicholas Knighte of Chawton. Co: Southampton.

To the parish Church of Chawton 20*s*. To the poor of the same parish 20*s*. To Mr. Hunt 10*s*. To the poore people within the parish of Alton 20*s*.

To my son Nicholas Knight & his heirs one yearly rent of £10 to be taken out of my manor of Lymester in Co: of Sussex to be paid Michaelmas & Lady Day first payment on which shall first happen after the said Nicholas shall come to 24 years.

To the said Nicholas if he shall come to 25 years £100 within 20 days after.

To my son Stephen & his heirs one yearly rent of £10 out of my manor of Lymester on the same conditions & £100 also.

To

To my son Henry Knight and his heirs one yearly rent of £10 out of the Manor of Lymester on the same conditions & £100 also.

To my daughter Jane £200 at 19 years within 20 days if married, or at the day of her marriage—or at 24 years, which first shall happen. To the said Jane £20 towards her wedding apparel.

To my daughter Mawde £200 on the same conditions. To the said Mawde £20 towards her wedding apparel.

To my daughter Elizabeth £200 on the same conditions. To the said Elizabeth £20 towards her wedding apparel.

To my daughter Ann £200 on the same conditions. To the said Ann £20 towards her wedding apparel.

My said daughters shall follow the counsel and advice of Thomas Henslowe & John Mersham Gentlemen in their marriages otherwise the said legacies shall not be paid until they have accomplished the several ages of 30 years.

If any of my said sons part with the said yearly rents before they come to their several ages of 24 years then the gift is to be void.

If any controversy prevents my sons from receiving their annuities out of the Manor of Lymester then they shall have them out of my Manor of Chawton Co: Southampton. To the said Stephen my son and his heirs the tenement and lands which Emerye Stronges holdeth of me in Lymester aforesaid the said Stephen to enter when he cometh 24 years.

To Henry Knighte and his heirs the tenement & land which John Alderslade doth dwell in and one house in Alton which one Jeffrey dwelleth in and two shops near unto the said house.

If the said gifts and lands & tenements be not good unto the said Stephen and Henry, then each of them to have £10 more yearly out of the said Manor of Lymester. If my wife be with manchild he shall have £20 yearly payable out of the said Manor of Lymester, if a woman child such portion as to the rest of my daughters I have given. My will is that my said sons Nicholas, Stephen and Henry shall be brought up in learning at the cost of my Executors until such time as they shall accomplish 24 years.

My

My mind is that my said daughters shall be brought up conveniently and orderly at the cost of my Executors until such time as they shall accomplish 19 years if married, if otherwise then until 24 years if in the meantime they do not marry.

I give and bequeath to my father & mother, or to either of them one old Royall willing and charging my Executors that they shall be very well used.

To my sister Thomasine Okeshott 40 shillings.

Unto every one of my servants 3s. 4d. Unto every one of my God children 12d. Unto the poor people of Anstie & Halliborne 6s. 8d.

And whereas I have demised and letten my Manor of Chawton Co: Southampton, the Rectory or parsonage of Barham Co: Sussex, all my lands & tenements in Chichester in said Co: the Manor of Todham Co: Sussex ; and all my lands in Alton Co: Southampton unto Thomas Henslowe of Borehunt Co: Southampton Gentleman for divers years yet enduring paying such yearly rents as have been mentioned, my will is that the said Thomas Henslowe shall receive the rents thereof & make a just account unto John Knighte my son and heir when he shall come to 24 years—that my said heir shall therewith pay my debts & legacies & portions—if the residue of my goods left to my Executors shall not suffice.

And whereas also I have demised and letten unto John Mersham all my said Manor of Lymester Co: Sussex for divers years yet enduring paying therefor yearly £20 the said John Mersham shall receive the rents to the intent he shall pay unto the Queen's Majesty for a 3rd part of the said Manor during the minority of the said John Knight and afterwards yield an account to my said heir.

My will is if Thomas Tompson and Avise his wife do make a whole release unto my said heir within ¼ of a year after my decease of such lands as were John Standens late of Lavant Co: Sussex deceased & now in possession of me or my tenant then Avise my daughter shall have £100 to be paid within 2 years after my decease.

I give to Thomas Henslowe one balde colte, unto John Mersham 40s. The residue of all my goods unto my son John Knight &
Elizabeth

Elizabeth my wife whom I make executors & the said Thomas Henslow & John Mersham Overseers.

In witness I have set my hand and seal the IX of October in the reign of our Lady Elizabeth 25.

Witnesses John Mersham Gent. William Hunch, Clerk & Thomas Newman.

Memorandum : I appoint William Knight of Farringdon and Robert Locke of Bensteede as two other overseers and to each of them 40s. this VII day of January, 26 Elizabeth.

APPENDIX VI

NOTE ON KNIGHT ARMS

Two coats of arms seem to have been borne by the family of Knight in the sixteenth century, viz. (1) per chevron argent and sable three cinquefoils counter changed ; (2) vert a bend lozengy or.

A manuscript at the College of Arms of the time of Henry VIII gives the first coat as the arms of Knight of Calais. The second coat was borne by Knight Norroy, King of Arms, who died 1593, and by Knight Chester Herald, who died 1618.

At the Visitation of London made in 1634 a pedigree of Knight was recorded with arms of the second coat, and these arms appear to have been granted by Sir William Segar, Garter, to Arthur Knight and Stephen Knight, both of London, gentlemen, sons of John Knight of Kelvedon, Co. Essex, and grandsons of William Knight of Calais.

After the Restoration there is a grant of a Royal Augmentation by Sir Edward Walker in which the arms of Knight are the two coats of the lozenges and cinquefoils quarterly with a St. George's Cross on an escutcheon cf pretence, which coat Guillim gives as the bearing of John Knight of Durham Yard in the parish of St. Martin in the Fields, principal chirurgeon to his Majesty King Charles the Second. John Knight, who was the first of the Chawton family to bear arms, sealed his letters with the bend lozengy.

His

His nephew Richard gave a silver flagon to the Church engraved with the same arms. His great-nephew Sir Richard had his arms blazoned on a panel still hanging in the Hall at Chawton, quartering the lozenges and cinquefoils with the Reynolds arms on an escutcheon of pretence ; but on his monument in the Church, as also on that of William Woodward Knight, the three cinquefoils are omitted, and only the bend lozengy appears for Knight. What connexion there was between the Chawton family and William Knight of Calais, the two Heralds, and King Charles the Second's principal chirurgeon, we are unable to trace.

The bend lozengy coat suffered the first loss of its original simplicity in 1738 when, on Thomas May's change of name under Mrs. Elizabeth Knight's will, a difference was made by the College of Arms and a cinquefoil argent was introduced in base.

A second change was made in 1812, when the arms were exemplified to Edward Austen on his change of name to Knight as vert a bend lozengy or in base a cinquefoil argent and (for distinction) a Canton gules.

The crest as granted by Sir William Segar is thus described : ' A demi Hermert or Fryar vested and hooded ar. having an upper mantle or and holding in his right hand a Lanterne or pourfiled or and in his left a Paternoster Gules y⁰ Crucifix pendant at the end.'

This is very much the crest on Sir Richard Knight's monument, except that the Paternoster has lost the final crucifix.

In 1738, on the succession of the Brodnaxes, a change was made —the lantern which had given light to the 'Night' was replaced by a cinquefoil taken from the Brodnax coat of arms, and the crest became a demi gray friar proper holding in his dexter hand a cinquefoil slipped ar. from the sinister wrist a bracelet of beads pendant sable.

A further change was made in 1812, when the breast was charged with a rose gules to mark the Austen connexion and the bracelet of beads is called a rosary.

The motto since 1679 has been—
Suivant St. Pierre.

APPENDIX VII

EXTRACTS FROM THE WILL OF JOHN KNIGHT

'IN the Name of God Amen. I John Knight of Chawton in the County of South'ton Esquire, doe make and ordeine this my last will and testament,' &c.

After giving for ever for the relief of the poor in Chawton-Warnford and Alton a yearly rent of Six Pounds out of Amery Farm, 'Item I give to my Brother Sir Thomas Neale, Knight a piece of plate of the value of tenne Pounds and the like to my sister his Ladie. Item to my kinswoman the Ladie Anne Brooke, the wife of Sir John Brooke, Knight, the Silver Tankard given me by my sister the Ladie Elizabeth Neale deceased. Item to my Brother Sir Francis Neale Kt. a piece of plate of the value of Six Pounds thirteen shillings and fourpence. Item to my Sister his Ladie, the like. To my kinswoman the Ladie Anne Brooke wife of Sir Thomas Brooke Kt. a piece of plate of the value of Six Pounds thirteen shillings and fourpence. To my kinswoman the Ladie Frances Cave the wife of Sir Thomas Cave Kt. a piece of plate of the value of Six Pounds thirteen shillings and fourpence. The like to my kinswoman Mrs. Mary Fisher the wife of Paine Fisher Esquire and to my kinswoman Mrs. Elizabeth Neale the daughter of the said Sir Thomas Neale. Item I give to my Sister Jones to bestow in plate £20 and the like to my Sister Avise Knight. Item to Mr. Doctor Cradocke a ring of 20 shillings. The like to Mr. Richard Mason the Minister of Chawton and also to Mr. Price the Minister of Warnford. Item to my kinsman Mr. Adryan Jugpen and Mr. William Jugpen to either of them 40 shillings. Item I give to every of the household Servants of my Brother Sir Thomas Neale that shall be dwelling and abiding with him at the time of my decease 20 shillings. To my Servant John Bernard Tenne Pounds—to my Servant Thomas Knight £6 13s. 4d.—I have promised that his wife shall have an estate during her life in the tenement his Mother

now

now dwelleth in and holdeth of me in Chawton the which I will to be performed. To my Servant William Knight Five Pounds and the tenement in Chawton the which he now dwelleth in and was lately Robert Knight deceased for the terme of his life, the said William yielding and paying therefor yearly during his life the ancient and accustomed rent. I will that Thomas Buckland doe hould and enjoy all the land and tenements that are now in his tenure and occupation in Chawton as well copyholds as others during the space of one year next after my decease if he shall so long live without paying any rent or other consideration during that time. Item I give and bequeath to either of the two daughters of my Sister Dawtrey deceased and to every one of the children of my Sister Muschampe likewise deceased begotten by my Brother Mr. Christopher Muschampe her late husband also deceased the sum of fifty Pounds to be paid to every of the daughters when they shall attain to their several ages of 19 years if married, if unmarried to be paid to them when they shall attain to their several ages of 21 and to be paid to the sonnes when they shall be 24 and in the meantime the said several sums of £50 to every of the said sonnes and daughters so given to be used and employed for their benefit and profit. If any of them should die before, his or her share to be divided among the rest.' He makes his Brother Stephen sole executor and residuary legatee.

'Additions to the last will of me John Knight. I revoke £20 of the legacie given in my will to my kinswoman Dawtrey, she that married with one Boyes. I think her name be Jane, for that I did give her a little before her marriage £22. So that my meaning is she shall have but £30.

'My meaning is that not any of those that belong to the Paper Mill shall be reckoned any of the household Servants of Sir Thomas Neale. Item I give my diamond ring that is commonly tied to my purse strings to my Sister Ladie Mary Neale and my black enameld ring that I usually wear on my little finger to my Sister the Ladie Honor Neale. Item I give to my kinswoman Elizabeth Neale, my greate plaine gould ringe weighing between forty and fifty

fifty shillings and on which is written vizt. Mori mihi lucrum.   Item
I give to my Servant Emmanuel Seward £20, and to my Servant
William Knight more than I have formerly given him £10.'

EXTRACTS FROM STEPHEN KNIGHT'S WILL

' To the poor of Chawton £10.   To my daughter Anne Knight
£600.   To my daughter Dorothy Knight £500 when she comes of
age.   To my daughter Frances Knight £500 when she comes of age.
Dorothy and Frances to receive £30 a year till they are of age.
To my son Richard £600 when he comes of age.   £20 yearly for
his maintenance till he be 17.   After that £30 yearly till he be 21.
Also a messuage and tenement and Lands lying in Lymester.'

His three daughters to have free ingress, egress and regress into
the House ' wherein I usually did lodge in Lincoln's Inn Fields so
long as my lease doth endure.'   A furnished lodging chamber each
until they shall otherwise dispose of themselves.

He makes ' my brother Richard Turner and my Nephew Christopher Muschampe ' executors during the minority of his son John.
After he has attained the age of 21 he is to be sole executor and
residuary legatee.

There is a codicil with a lot of additional legacies :
'To Blithman Parson of Chawton 40s. to buy him a ring.
To my brother Jones 20s. for the like.
To my Brother John Knight 20s. for the like.
To my brother Turner 40s.
To my nephew Christopher Muschampe 40s.
Also to buy him a Nagge £10.
To my nephew William's daughter £5,' &c., &c.

APPENDIX VIII

AN INVENTARY of the Goods & Chattells of Sr. Richard Knight
late of Chawton in the County of Southton Knight—dec'd. taken
& apprised the 16 day of September Anno Dni 1679 by Mr. Thomas
Townsend William Fisher Thomas Mathew & Edward Fisher.

Imprimis

Imprimis his wearing Apparell & money in the
house   ..   ..

In the Hall

Item two long tables one round table three formes   £   *s.*   *d.*
one sideboard two Andirons and a Back   1   0   0

In the Dyneing Roome

Item two wooden tables two Stone tables & frames
two dozen of turkey worke chaires one turky worke
Carpett eight large pictures whereof fower in guilded
frames & fower in black frames one paire of large
brasse Andirons one paire of doggs firepan & tongs
one large Lookeing glasse fower white worsted window
Curtaines & Curtaine Rodds   10   0   0

In the passage from ye Hall to the Dyneing
Roome

Item one stone table and frame three Mapps whereof one of the Manno^r of Chawton and two stone
heads on pillars   1   10   0

In the little chamber over ye Dyneing-roome

Item one feather bedd & bedsted bolster & pillows
a paire of blanketts & a redd rugg strip'd curtains
Vallens & Hangings—three wooden turned chaires
a small table & lookeing glasse a paire of iron doggs &
tongs   1   10   0

In the other Chamber over the Dineing roome

Item fower stooles two elbowe chaires & a little
table two Andirons with brasse nobbs   0   5   0

In the passage over the Dyneing roome staires

Item three spanish tables and a sideboard   0   6   8

In

2 D

	£	s.	d.

In the little Chamb. at yᵉ staire head there
Item two feather beds one bolster one pillow one
bedsted one table and frame and two chaires a paire
of blankets and a browne Rugg   2   0   0

In the Grey Chamber
Item one feather bed and Bedsted one bolster two
pillows two blanketts one redd coverlet Curtains &
double valens with silke fring a Counterpane & window
Curtains of grogarin seaven chairs one stool lyned &
one table Carpett of the same stuffe two tables & two
stands a large lookeing glasse a paire of brass Andirons
with broad heads a paire of iron doggs firepan & tongs   3   0   0

In the purple Chamber over the Hall
Item one feather bedd a bolster & pillowe a paire
of blanketts a quilt Curtaines double Valens a Counterpane three peeces of tapestry hangings five purple
wrote chaires and three Stooles suiteable to the bedd
two twisted iron doggs one small table white callicoe
window curtaines & curtain Rodd   8   0   0

In the passage betwixt the two staire Cases
Item one side board a Redd Stoole & a twisted
wooden couch   0   3   4

In the passage at the parloʳ staircase head
Item one chimed clock & case three pictures where-
of one large & two small ones   5   0   0

In the Chamber over the Parloʳ
Item four peeces of Tapestry hangings four
callicoe window curtaines two rodds a feather bed
bolster a paire of blankets a quilt & moohaire Curtaines & double Valens lyned with red Sasenett & a
Counterpane of the same quilted & fringed six
chaires suiteable to the Curtaines a table & a paire
of Stands a paire of twisted andirons a paire of doggs
a twisted fire pan & tongs and one other firepan   ..   20   0   0

In

	£	s.	d.

In the Closet by
Item a table Bedsted a quilt a boulster a blankett
and rugg 0 10 0

In the Chamber over the Buttery
Item a feather bedd one boulster a paire of blankets
a quilt a bedsted & Connlett furniture two great
chaires six lowe chaires a Counterpane two paire of
brasse doggs fire pan & tongs four calicoe window
curtains & Rodds and a lowe table 10 0 0

In ye chamber over ye Kitchen
Item one feather bedd two boulsters one pillow a
paire of Blanketts @ green Rugg curtains & valens one
large wainscott chest a large wainscott presse a
spanish table 2 10 0

In the Chamber over the Wellhouse
Item five pieces of Tapestry hangings one feather
bedd one boulster one Counterpane four serge Curtaines lyned two Turkey worke Carpetts one stand ..   5 0 0

In the Chamber over ye Larder
Item two feather bedds one boulster a rugg with
curtains and valens 2 0 0

Lynnen
Item six & twenty paire of Sheets whereof two
paire are Holland fourteen paire flaxen and the rest
are Canvasse 8 0 0
Item two table clothes and two dozen of napkins
of Hollan Dyaper 1 10 0
Item nyne dozen & a halfe of napkins & two &
twenty table clothes & sideboard clothes of ordinary
Dyaper & seaven towells of the same 8 0 0
Item one dozen of course table clothes & five
dozen & an half of course napkins 2 10 0

                                                                Plate

	£	s.	d.

Plate

Mem. Lady Knight own'd a sylver Tankard before Mrs. Brickenden on y⁰ 1st of May 1704.

Item one large silver Bason four tumblers and Sugar box one pepper box one Mustard Box two porringers one hand candlestick a paire of table candlesticks Ten spoons seaven forkes and one guilt Cawdle Cupp 23 3 4

In the Garrett Chambs.
Item fower bedds & bedstedles with the app'tences thereto belonging 2 13 4

In the Garrett over the parlo\
Item one feather bedd boulster a pare of blanketts a rugg Curtaines & valens one Chaire five stooles & a table a paire of Andirons fire pan & tongs 2 0 0

In the Parlo\ Starecase
Item four pictures 0 4 0

In the Parlo\
Item one round table two side tables sixteen Cane Chaires one Cane Couch a Pendulum Watch & case fower Callicoe window curtaines & rodds & five pictures a pair of brasse Andirons fire pan & tongs 5 0 0

In the Gravell Garden
Item two Statues with their pedestalls .. ..

Item in other places abroad by the house three marble stone tables .. ..

Item one brasse clock in y⁰ passage from the Hall to the Kitchen 1 0 0

In the Brewhouse
Item one large copper Furnace and Meshing fatt two Tuns one Cooler five Kivers one long tubb and other small utensills 5 0 0

In

	£	s.	d.

In the Buttery

Item one round table and frame one double Been
& a napkin presse   0   10   0

In the owter Sellar

Item three & twenty hogsheads & fower Stands ..   6   0   0

In the middle Sellar

Item seaven hogsheads three Ale vessells & three
stands   2   0   0

In the Kitchen
Pewter

Item two dozen and fower pewter dishes seaven
large plates al's Mazarins fower intermesses three pye
plates three dozen & nyne trencher plates nyne
candlesticks six chamber potts & Cesterne   5   0   0

Brasse & Iron

Item five Kettles fower potts four skilletts fower
sawcepans two candlesticks & two warming pans ..   5   0   0
Item fower spitts and Spitt-Jack two dripping pans
one iron grate or rack three Cottrells two other racks   2   0   0

In severall roomes in the House

Item two needleworke carpetts one couch & a
dozen of needle worke chairs all suiteable   1   10   0

APPENDIX IX

PLAN OF CHAWTON COMMON WITH THE ALLOTMENTS.
　　　Do.　　SOUTH FIELD IN COMMON.
　　　　　　SOUTH FIELD ALLOTMENTS.
　　　Do.　　NORTH FIELD IN COMMON.
　　　　　　NORTH FIELD ALLOTMENTS.
　　　Do.　　RIDGE FIELD IN COMMON.
　　　　　　RIDGE FIELD ALLOTMENTS.
　　　　　　WHITE DOWN AND WINSTREET ALLOTMENTS.
　　　Do.　　UPPER EAST FIELD IN COMMON.
　　　　　　UPPER EAST FIELD ALLOTMENTS.
　　　Do.　　LOWER EAST FIELD IN COMMON.
　　　　　　LOWER EAST FIELD ALLOTMENTS.

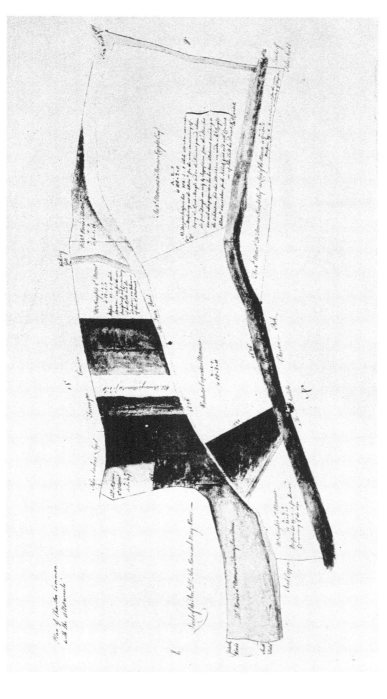

PLAN OF CHAWTON COMMON WITH THE ALLOTMENTS

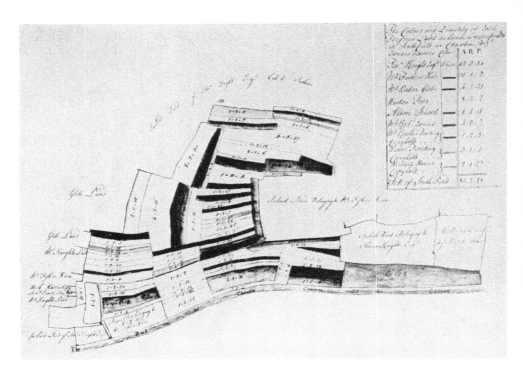

SOUTH FIELD IN COMMON

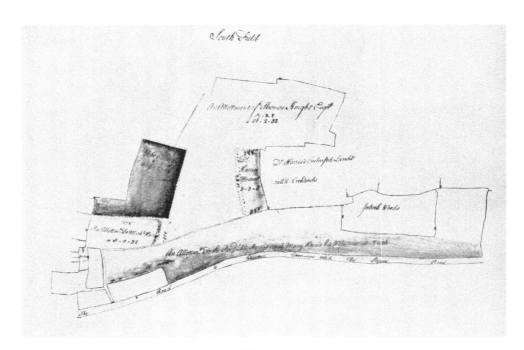

SOUTH FIELD ALLOTMENTS

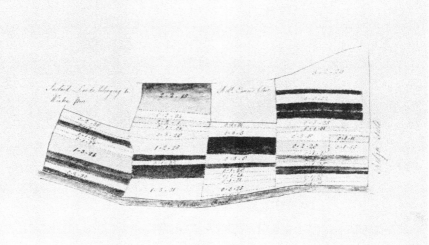

NORTH FIELD IN COMMON

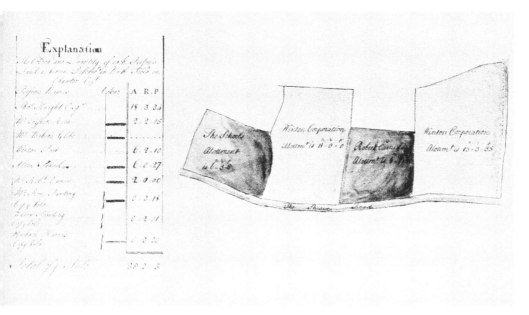

NORTH FIELD ALLOTMENTS

2 E

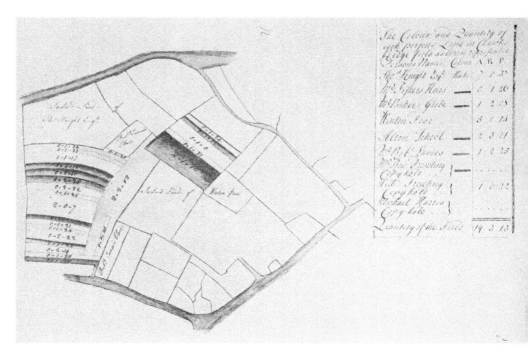

RIDGE FIELD IN COMMON

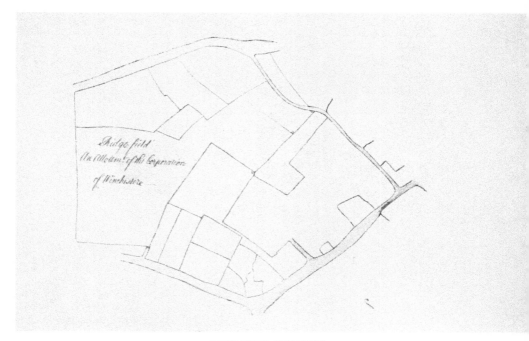

RIDGE FIELD ALLOTMENTS

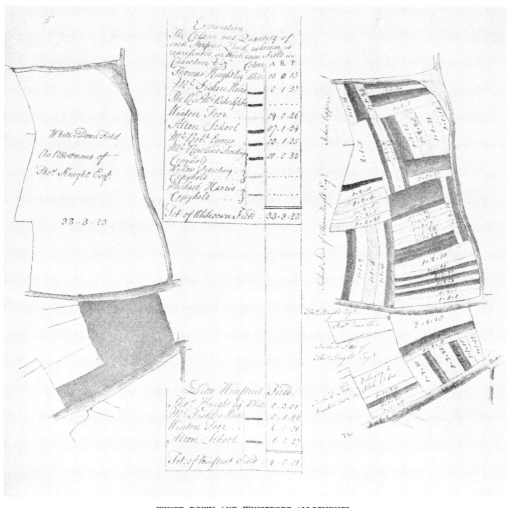

WHITE DOWN AND WINSTREET ALLOTMENTS

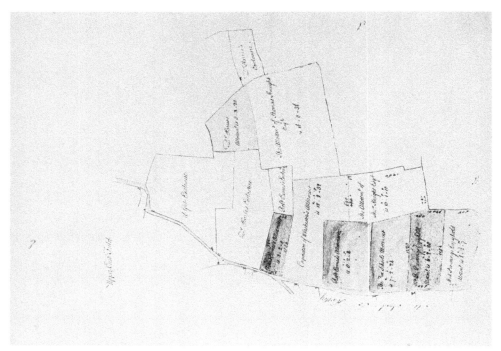

UPPER EAST FIELD ALLOTMENTS

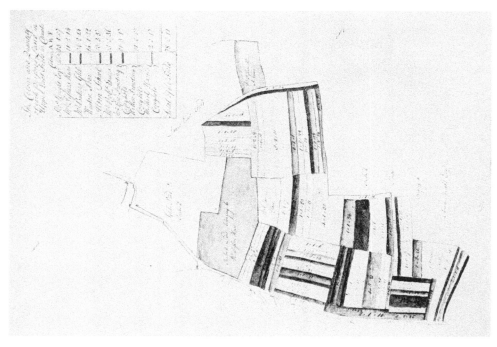

UPPER EAST FIELD IN COMMON

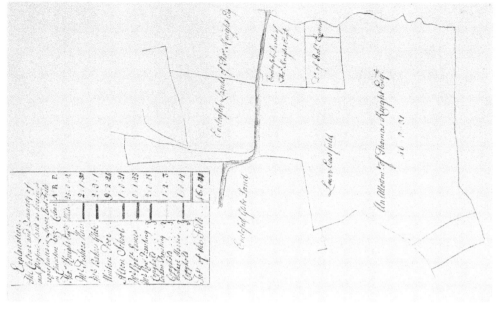

LOWER EAST FIELD ALLOTMENTS

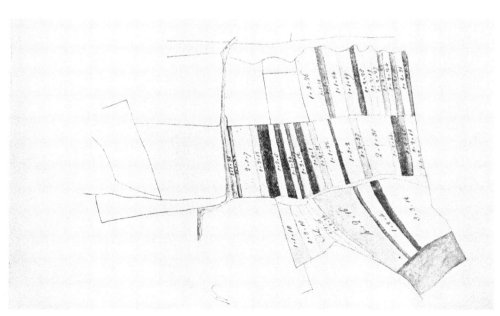

LOWER EAST FIELD IN COMMON

INDEX

ALTON, Pass of, 14–16

Arundel, Thomas, purchases manorial rights of Chawton in 1558, and sells them in 1578, 6, 76

Austen, family, settled at Horsmonden in Kent, owning Broadford and Grovehurst houses, 152; account of children of John Austen and Elizabeth Weller, 153–155; marriage of Jane Austen to Stephen Stringer, 156; their grand-daughter Jane (Monke) married to Thomas Knight (I), 8, 156

Austen, Frank, befriends his nephews, 154; his descendants now own the family property, 152, 154

Austen, William, fourth son of John Austen and Elizabeth Weller, marries Rebecca Walter (Hampson), 155; their children, George and Philadelphia (Hancock), 155

Austen, (Rev.) George, Fellow of St. John's College, Oxford, and proctor, 155; marries Cassandra Leigh, 9, 157; Rector of Steventon, on presentation of Thomas Knight (I), 8, 156; his son Edward adopted by Thomas Knight (II), 8, 157, 158; dies at Bath, 166

Austen, Cassandra, mutual affection of Cassandra and Jane, 10, 164

Austen, Jane, birth, 161; education, partly away from home, 163; romance in the West, 168; abandons writing for some years, 168; settles at Chawton, and resumes writing, 10, 168; description of her appearance, 167; her books published, 168, 169; secluded life there, 169; her letters to Cassandra misunderstood, 164; family troubles, illness, and death, 10, 170, 171

Austen, (Rev.) James, succeeds his father at Steventon, 160, 166; his son (Rev.) James Edward Austen Leigh, 160

Austen, Edward. See Knight, Edward (I)

Austen, (Rev.) Henry, favourite brother of Jane, 160, 163; fails in business, 170; takes Orders, 160; his letter about Chawton Church, 61

Austen, (Sir) Francis, Admiral of the Fleet, 160

Austen, Charles, Admiral, 160

BEAN, old family at Chawton, 32, Appendix I

Bonville, family own Chawton, 4

Bridges, Elizabeth. See Knight, Edward (I)

highly praised by Hasted, 146. *See also* Brodnax family : May family : Knight, Elizabeth

Knight, Thomas (II), his character and love for Oxford, 147; M.P., marries Catherine Knatchbull, 148; pictures of him and wife by Romney, frontispiece, 149; appreciation by a friend, 148; adopts Edward Austen, and leaves property to him, 9, 159

Knight, Edward (I) (Edward Austen), adopted by Mr. T. Knight (II), 9; travels abroad, 158–159 ; marries Elizabeth Bridges, 159 ; death of his wife, 159 ; settles mother and sisters at Chawton, 166; threatened claim on Hants property compromised, 171 ; dies at Godmersham, 1852, 172. *See also* Austen, (Rev.) George

Knight, Edward (II), succeeds his father, 173 ; lives at Chawton and sells Godmersham, 173 ; marries (1) Mary Dorothea Knatchbull, (2) Adela Portal, 173 ; portrait by Grant, 173 ; account of him in *Hampshire Chronicle* on his death, 1879, 173 ; account of his brothers and sisters, 172

LA WARR, Lord, owns Chawton, 4, 22; letter of, respecting sale of land to John Knight, 75

Leigh, Cassandra. *See* Austen, (Rev.) George

Lewkenor, family, pedigree, 96 ; settled at Westdean, 97; monument there, 97. *See also* Carpet of Arms

Lewkenor, Christopher, marries Mary May, 115; attempts in vain to hold Chichester for Charles I, 98; report to King, 99 *et seq.*; King's answer, 113; knighted, 116 ; helps to defend Fort Charles,

116 ; abroad, 117 ; daughters recover portions from Crown, one marries Woodward, one marries Martin, 117

Lewkenor, Sir John, nephew of Christopher, marries Ann Mynne, 117; correspondence on tests, 117 ; on James II and Fellows of Magdalen, 118 ; on birth of Prince, 121; on flight of James II, 121 ; Sir John's son John dies without issue, and leaves property to W. Woodward and Elizabeth Knight, 127

MAGDALEN College, Oxford, Fellows of, withstand James II, 118 *et seq.*

Manor (*see* Chapter II) given by William I to Hugh de Port, 4, 17–19; account in Domesday Book, 17–19; family take the name of St. John, 19; medieval documents quoted, 22, 24, 25, 26; ownership continues in female line till sixteenth century, 20–22; Nicholas Knight purchases Manor, 76; account of demesne lands at that date, 46; account of Courts, 28 *et seq.* ; Enclosure Act, 1740–1741, 47–50

Martin, family, their home in Oxon, and coat of arms, 122–123 ; intermarriage with Knights, 7, 122; Michael Martin saves Chawton woods, 123; marries Frances Lewkenor, 122 ; their three children own Chawton in succession, 123–124

May, family, younger branch settle in Portugal, 133 ; return and acquire Rawmere, 133 ; influential positions in seventeenth century, 133–138 ; failure of male heirs and descent of property to Brodnaxes, 142. *See also* Hicks, Baptist : Knight, Thomas (I) : Lewkenor, Christopher. For Pashly branch *see* May, Thomas

THE END

PRINTED BY
SPOTTISWOODE AND CO. LTD., COLCHESTER
LONDON AND ETON

For EU product safety concerns, contact us at Calle de José Abascal, 56–1°,
28003 Madrid, Spain or eugpsr@cambridge.org.

www.ingramcontent.com/pod-product-compliance
Ingram Content Group UK Ltd.
Pitfield, Milton Keynes, MK11 3LW, UK
UKHW010037140625
459647UK00012BA/1435